SHOPPING FOR CHURCH

SEARCHING FOR CHRISTIAN COMMUNITY, A
MEMOIR

VISITING CHURCHES SERIES
BOOK 4

PETER DEHAAN

Library of Congress Control Number: 2023904775

Published by Rock Rooster Books, Grand Rapids, Michigan

ISBNs:

- 979-8-88809-041-1 (e-book)
- 979-8-88809-042-8 (paperback)
- 979-8-88809-043-5 (hardcover)
- 979-8-88809-044-2 (audiobook)

Credits:

- Developmental editor: Julie Harbison
- Copy editor: Robyn Mulder
- Cover design: Taryn Nergaard
- Author photo: Chelsie Jensen Photography

To Luke Bilberry

Books in the Visiting Churches Series

52 Churches
More Than 52 Churches
Visiting Online Church
Shopping for Church
The 52 Churches Workbook
The More Than 52 Churches Workbook

For a list of all Peter's books, go to
    PeterDeHaan.com/books

CONTENTS

CHURCH SHOPPING

My wife and I are looking for a new church. I never thought we'd be in this situation. My assumption was we'd go to our church for the rest of our lives. So much for assumptions.

While writing my not-yet-published memoir, *God, I Don't Want to Go to Church*, I realized I'd picked every church Candy and I have attended over the years. I'd have my favorite; she'd have hers. Unable to agree, I'd effectively decide because I drove. She'd go along, grumbling a bit as we went, but eventually we'd settle into life at our new church.

For our last church, I committed us to be part of a church plant without consulting her. I assumed she'd be as excited as me. I was wrong. Eventually she embraced my choice as we immersed ourselves with giddy excitement into the allure of creating a fresh faith expression, working with a like-minded community of spiritual mavericks and misfits, rejects of today's church culture.

I later apologized to her for always picking our churches. I promised she could pick the next one—even though I assumed there never would be a next one.

A few years later, after our yearlong sabbatical of researching and writing *52 Churches*, we returned to our home church. We picked up where we left off. Friends welcomed us back, excited about our return. A few, however, never knew we were gone. This reminded me of how big and disconnected our church had become. Faithful regulars, even with a visible presence each Sunday, could slip away for a year and not be missed.

In his book *The Barbarian Way*, Erwin McManus wrote about being barbarians for Jesus, of not settling for a civilized acceptance of the religious status quo. We started our church plant as passionate barbarians, but in eight short years we had settled into a civilized acquiescence. We had become like other churches, just with edgier music and more attendees from society's fringe.

As we became organized (civilized), there was less room for my maverick soul to find solace. An all-too-familiar ache resurfaced, that spiritual yearning for more. This unanswered pang in my spirit left me again asking questions about what it means to truly follow Jesus and how his church should function. Church is not to assure our comfort, but to insure his kingdom.

Our daughter and her family went to this church with us. We persisted in attending to be with them. But then our son-in-law switched jobs, and they moved near our son and his wife.

The pull of family caused us to ask an unexpected question: Should we move too? After consulting with our kids and receiving their blessing, we did just that.

Now we need to find a new church.

I desire to worship with our neighbors in our new community, so we'll look at churches nearby. Yet most of their buildings and names suggest they're traditional congregations, with traditional views, and little patience for nontraditional me.

We'll also consider the churches our neighbors attend. As far as we know, most of them drive outside our community each Sunday. If one of these churches clicks, at least we'll be able to attend with *some* neighbors.

A third consideration is our kids' churches. However, our daughter and son-in-law are still looking, while I'm not sure how long our son and daughter-in-law will continue where they're going. What are the chances we could all end up at the same place?

We'll know the right church when we see it, but it's good to have an idea of what we're looking for.

For me, true community is paramount. This implies a smaller congregation. I also want a church family that goes all out to follow Jesus, worships the Father in spirit and in truth, and embraces the power of the Holy Spirit. I need a truly Trinitarian faith community. Traditional churches need not apply.

In addition, it's important to find a church that gives me a place to plug in and help others. Over the years I've served in many areas at the churches we've attended, often in excess and to the detriment of my family. At one time I was simultaneously involved in ten different areas at our church, going there two or three times throughout the week to meet all my commitments, in addition to being quite busy on Sundays.

Over the years I've served as elder, deacon, treasurer, assistant treasurer, and executive committee member. A few times I even gave the sermon. I also headed up one church's small group ministry, a 20-hour-a-week commitment. I've taught various Sunday school classes, from preschool to adult, with the junior high boys being my favorite. Along the way, I've led small groups. Then there is ushering, greeting, and taking the collection. And I've been on more commit-tees than I care to remember.

Though I could do any of these things again, I don't feel God calling me to any of them at this time. I also don't think these are the *best* way for me to help advance his Kingdom.

After too many years of overcommitment, I established a guideline for my church involvement. It works well. Quite simply, in addition to the Sunday service, I'm open to do one additional thing each week—and only one thing—at church. That's it. I hope the church we pick offers me this one place to serve, one that will give me life.

Candy's list is different. She seeks music that is

worshipful and not a performance. They must speak the truth but in love. Last, she wants a church willing to address today's issues, not worrying about being politically correct or afraid to declare biblical truth.

In visiting congregations for *52 Churches*, I set each destination with only minimal input from my wife. It was my research. We weren't looking for a new church, so the consequences were minimal.

This time is different. We're seeking a new church home. The stakes are high. This won't be a methodical investigation to gather information. It's an imperative journey to find a new church family, a place for us to belong.

This time we'll make the list together. I expect we'll skip traditional congregations, formal gatherings, and liturgical services. While these are ideal choices for some, they have no pull for us.

Though this journey is ours together, and I will write the book from my perspective, Candy will make the final decision. I promised her that. My hope is I'll be able to accept her selection and then embrace it, just as she did with my past choices.

Our journey to find a new church home is about to begin.

THE PORTABLE CHURCH
A DIFFERENT APPROACH

As we transition between homes, we're living with our son and daughter-in-law. We'll go to Sunday services with them, holding off on our search for a new church home. We've already gone with them a handful of times over the past few years, and for this season in our lives, it will be more regularly.

Now, each Sunday morning, we all hop in the car and head to church. It's a nondenominational gathering, about ten years old. The congregation includes people of all ages, though it skews toward young families. Notably, the church doesn't own a building. It rents space for their Sunday service, meeting in a well-known banquet hall. I like that they aren't spending money on a mortgage and building maintenance for a facility used only a few hours each week. This frees up funds to help people in need and reach out to the community.

This modern, well-maintained facility is easy to get to,

with ample parking near the door. Though designed as a banquet hall and conference center, it adapts nicely for church, with a large meeting space for the service and other areas for children's activities. In their typical Sunday configuration, the meeting space seats about three hundred, with padded chairs arrayed in four sections. Attendance varies, between 70 percent occupied to near capacity.

Early each Sunday morning, a setup team prepares the place for church. They arrange chairs provided by the facility and lay out their service-related items, which they unpack and repack each week. A trailer specifically designed for this purpose transports these items on Sunday and stores them between services. Though set up and tear down have many steps, transforming the space and then returning it to its default condition goes quickly with many volunteers.

There is sometimes a greeter by the main entrance and always a pair by the main door of the worship space. They pass out brochures that function as mini newsletters, sharing little about the service and more about activities going on throughout the week.

The people dress casually. I see no men in suits or even wearing ties. Though a few women wear dresses, there aren't many. The common attire is jeans. They're also a friendly group. We've met many people but are still waiting to form connections because we seldom see the same people from one week to the next. This is partly because of the number of people attending. However, a bigger factor, I suspect, is that most of the people are inconsistent with their attendance. They have competing options for Sunday morning, and church doesn't always win out.

To start the service, the worship team sings an opening song. They never display the lyrics so we can't sing or even follow along unless we know the words. Most of the regulars treat this first song with indifference, continuing their conversations. For the second song, the words appear on a large overhead screen, and most people redirect their attention and sing along. There are, however, people who stand mute during the singing. They don't even bother to move their lips. I'm sure this happens at all churches, but it seems more common here.

The members of the worship team vary from week to week, but they usually have six: the worship leader on keyboard, two guitars, a bass guitar, drums, and a backup vocalist—the only female in the group. With a light rock sound, they lead us in singing contemporary songs. Accomplished at what they do, the outcome is pleasing, but it's just like most any other contemporary church service.

At some point, a staff person gives announcements, and then a greeting time follows. They do well at welcoming one another, certainly better than most churches. But most conversations are brief, as the number of people greeted takes precedence over the depth of conversation: quantity trumps quality.

About a half hour into the service, the minister stands for the first time, signaling a transition into the message. With a charismatic presence, this thirty-something pastor exudes confidence with an easygoing smile and approachable demeanor.

A peer of the congregation's largest demographic, he greets attendees and then prays before teaching. Sometimes he starts his message with an anecdote, while other times he opens by reading the Scripture text after a brief introduction. Words appear on the large screen overhead as he reads the passage.

A pop culture aficionado, he often weaves modern-day references into his messages to make his points. He also frequently uses visual aids in the form of handheld props or graphics displayed overhead.

This church is far too trendy for a traditional altar call, but the pastor ends his message with a more serious time of personal application or reflection. The service ends with a closing song and offering.

Afterward, most people stay and mingle. Longer conversations happen, and connections can occur. Donuts and beverages are available to entice people to stay and talk. But there are no tables or places to sit, so interaction must occur while standing. As conversations continue, the teardown crew gathers equipment and breaks down the stage. They reload the trailer, preparing it for next week when they'll do it again.

This is an easy church to attend, but I don't get a sense of spiritual depth or feel commitment from most of the people. I could easily amass acquaintances here, but friendships would require work. Though I'm open to attending this church, I don't think it's the one Candy will pick.

Takeaway: Seek to form genuine friendships and not merely make acquaintances.

THE MEGACHURCH
NAVIGATING BIG

O ur son and daughter-in-law's Sunday plans change abruptly one Sunday morning. We scramble to find a church to visit. Not just any church—that would be easy—but a church fitting our search criteria. However, we've not yet given it much thought. With little time to plan and most services already in progress, we need one that starts later.

A nearby megachurch has a second service at 11:30 a.m. We'll go there. One of our future neighbors attends this church, but the chances of spotting them in a crowd of thousands in the service we attend seems slim. Though big is not what I claim to want, the one church out of *52 Churches* that I felt the most affinity with, the one I sensed was the best match, was also the biggest. I hope this megachurch will evoke a similar connection.

We don't leave as soon as we should have. It will take a miracle to arrive on time, let alone ten minutes early, which is my goal when visiting churches. I pray aloud as we head their way. "God, slow my racing heart. May our focus be on you. May we worship you in spirit and in truth. Show us what you would have us to see. Teach us what you would have us to learn. May we give to others what you would have us to give. Amen."

"The speed limit is forty-five," Candy says. My heart still races, and our car's speed reveals it. I wonder how much of my prayer she heard and how much I meant. I sigh.

Taking my foot off the accelerator, I add something to my prayer. "Please don't let the service start until we get there." It's a selfish thing to ask, to assume God will make a couple thousand people wait because we didn't leave soon enough. Yet I don't know what else to pray. I need to slow down, both mentally and physically. Drawing in a deep breath as our car slows, I sigh again.

Now traveling at the posted speed, I accept the fact that we'll be late. For *52 Churches* we were never late once. But for this round, we'll be late on the first Sunday. It's not a good start.

We've been to their sprawling facility before, but it was for concerts in their youth center. We're not even sure where their sanctuary is. I follow the stream of cars. Parking attendants direct us to a general area. I follow the car in front of us and park next to it.

There's no clear path to the building and no obvious flow of people to follow. Some go right and others go left, while a few meander. We're already five minutes late and still must hike to the building. We're panting by the time we reach the doors.

Inside, activity bustles. Sounds come from all directions, with the loudest emanating from the right, but to the left is music and a doorway hinting that a sanctuary might be behind it.

Though twenty feet away, I make eye contact with a woman at the information center. I point to my left and, with raised eyebrows, mouth the question, "That way?"

Confused, she asks, "For what?"

"Is the sanctuary that way?"

She nods, and I veer left. Candy follows. I push forward.

Inside, the service is in full swing. My senses overload. I could aim for a seat in the back, but there's plenty of room closer to the front. I turn and head for the next aisle. Moving forward, we walk past twenty or more rows. Still well back from the stage, I slide into a seat near the aisle. Candy slips in beside me.

Astonished, I try to take it all in. I count fourteen on the worship team: guitars, drums, keys, and a slew of vocalists. Behind them sways a praise choir of twenty or thirty, smiling broadly, worshiping God with their singing and the gentle rhythm of their bodies. Overhead, three large screens, perhaps twenty or even thirty feet across, present the service in super-sized reality. Images of the worship team fill the giant displays with the song lyrics underneath. *Oh yeah, I'm supposed to be singing.*

I don't know the song but pick it up easily enough. However, as I look about, I soon stop singing. There are two boom cameras, whose constant motion distracts me, along with two handheld cameras roaming the stage in their operators' skilled hands. Two more stationary cameras round out the count to six. But from the various shots I see on the screens, there are even more cameras that I can't locate.

They continue to sing, but with too many distractions, I can't focus. After several songs, the worship leader asks the prayer teams to come forward. People seeking prayer follow them. As the prayer teams minister to those in need, the rest of us resume singing.

Eventually, a man I assume is the minister appears on stage. The worship team withdraws into the shadows. He reads Genesis 12:2–3. The words appear on the screens beneath his jumbo-sized image. I like this passage and often ask God to bless me so I can be a blessing to others. As I take notes, I assume this is the message, but he is simply introducing the offering.

As we resume our singing, ushers come down the center aisle, balancing stacks of buckets in their arms. They give one to each row as they work their way toward the back. As the buckets move across their rows, they accumulate offerings. In the adjacent aisles, more ushers pass the buckets across the chasm to the outside sections. On the end aisles, a final set of ushers receives the proceeds, struggling even more with their balancing act. Once completed, we stand again while we sing.

By now the main floor is mostly full, while the balcony is mostly empty. I wonder if there were more people at the first service. It's mid-August, so I suspect attendance is low. *How full will it be in another month?* I calculate the main level seats about 2,000, and surely the balcony holds at least 1,000 more, but both estimates could be off.

When the music ends, the worship leader tells us to greet

four or five people around us. Though smiles abound as we shake hands, there's little connection as the people move through this ritual with mechanical precision. I've only greeted three people when most others begin to sit. I turn to the two people behind me, not because I'm complying with the instruction to greet five people, but to push back at the brevity of the greeting time and its insignificance.

The minister returns. "What is the purpose of church?" He bounces through a series of Bible verses. I try to note them as I jot down some intriguing phrases: "The kingdom is here, within you," "Jesus wants disciples," and "All religions are men reaching out to God. Christianity is God reaching out to man."

An unassuming individual, the pastor doesn't look the part of a megachurch leader. Though confident, he lacks the polish I expect and the dynamic delivery I anticipate. Either his message lacks significance or I lack focus. Yet I can't shake the persistent feeling that our late arrival has seriously skewed my perceptions. We'll need to make a return visit for a proper experience. I've wasted our time today, failing to worship God or serve his people. I scan the crowd periodically, searching for our neighbors. I don't spot them.

"We focus on the receiving aspect of faith," says the minister as he wraps up his message, "but we also have a faith that sacrifices, a faith that gives." We watch a video about their TV ministry. The recording shows several people in India who are now following Jesus because of watching this church's services online each Sunday.

The video ends, and the congregation shows their affirmation with applause. Now they take a second offering, this one to support their TV ministry, which was the apparent underlying intent of the message. As the ushers return with their buckets to repeat their earlier performance, a series of video announcements play. The presenters are not mere talking heads, but polished announcers, comfortable in front of a camera, with an affable presence and the practiced cadence of a professional newscaster. I'm so impressed with the quality of their delivery that I miss their messages—all except one.

When we pulled into the facility, we had joked about a sign that simply read "Kids Sale" and gave dates. "How many kids do you want to buy?" I asked my wife.

"I wonder if you can sell kids too?" she quipped.

Now a video plug for this event repeats the same information but gives no clarification. It's still funny to me. "Do you want to buy one kid or two?"

"I think we have enough."

I want to give her a snappy comeback, but the service ends before I can. Everyone stands and files out. None of the people we greeted have any parting words to share, and I can't make eye contact with them. No one lingers to talk. Everyone exits the sanctuary, flowing as a mass of people intent on leaving.

The parking lot will be a mess, and we're in no hurry to be part of it. After using the restroom, Candy wonders aloud if there's a bulletin. I scoff. "This doesn't seem like a bulletin kind of church." But she heads over to the welcome center, now unstaffed, and proudly returns with a bulletin of sorts. In it we later learn that "Kids Sale" is a consignment sale of kids' games, clothes, and paraphernalia.

I consider heading over to a pavilion for "first-time visitors," something I spotted on the way in but skipped because of our tardiness. There's not much going on there, and I lack the motivation. Instead, we turn the other way and head outside, with our newly acquired bulletin in hand.

Walking just ahead of us is Vanessa, who sat in front of us at church, the only person whose name we know, learning it during our greeting time. I consider calling to her and wishing her a good afternoon. But she seems intent on leaving. Besides, we'll never see her again. I remain silent, even though I shouldn't. Frustrated, I just want to go home.

We walk at a leisurely pace back to our car, much slower than when we arrived. A warm sun and gentle breeze make it an enjoyable saunter. This should relax me but not quite. A line of cars still awaits their turn to leave. "I think there's a back way," Candy says.

"Let's try." I follow a couple of cars headed in the opposite direction. We wind our way through a maze of buildings, trees, and drives. "I don't know where we're going, but at least we're making good time."

Candy either ignores my quip or doesn't catch my humor. Eventually we find ourselves at a major road. It wasn't the one I expected, but it will work out even better.

Reviewing what happened, I'm discouraged: we arrived late, were distracted by most of the service, struggled to worship God, couldn't follow the sermon, failed to experience community, and didn't give anything to anyone. Vanessa was my one possibility, but I didn't even try.

I am empty, all the while knowing we'll need to make a return visit to consider this church. Next time we'll plan better. "Today was a complete waste."

My bride says nothing.

Takeaway: How you approach church influences your experience. If you leave empty, you likely failed to arrive prepared.

THE OUTLIER CONGREGATION
NEW APPROACHES FOR AN OLD DENOMINATION

I t's a holiday weekend. Our son and daughter-in-law are out of town, so we're free agents. A return trip to *The Megachurch* is in order, but our daughter invites us to go to a church she and her husband have visited the past couple of weeks. A friend from college invited her. *The Megachurch* can wait.

This church, part of an old traditional denomination, has two services: 9:15 and 11:00. We'll go to the first one. I check their website and am encouraged to read the bold proclamation: "Making passionate followers of Jesus." This must be their vision. Their mission statement likewise impresses me, using the phrases "community of faith," "renewed by the Holy Spirit," "transformation of lives and community," and "for God's glory."

Besides typical church components such as student ministries and community service opportunities, they also offer Alpha classes and small groups. What's unusual is they have a recovery program for people struggling with life issues. From what I see online, this is a big emphasis of this church.

I learn that the church is 7.2 miles away and the drive will take eleven minutes. We plan to leave twenty-five minutes early, but it ends up being more like fifteen. As I drive, Candy prays for our time there. Along the way, we pass several churches. As we wonder about them, the names become jumbled, and we forget the name of where we're headed. I should have written it down, along with the address. All I remember is the cross streets it's near. I hope there's only one church at that intersection.

But we find the church easily enough.

The facility is much larger than I expect. As we head toward the entrance, our daughter texts us they're running late. A young couple notices us, and the wife greets us. It's our daughter's friend from college. I've only seen her twice, with the last time being about three years ago, but she recognizes us right away.

We chat as we stroll into the building. They invite us to sit with them—if we'd like. We appreciate this friendly gesture and gladly accept, as they find seats for us and two more for the rest of our family. I estimate the sanctuary—which is a newer building with a trendy minimalist church design—seats four to five hundred. It's over half full, which isn't bad for a Labor Day weekend.

The service starts a few minutes late, but not before our kids arrive and slide in next to Candy. Soon the worship team—consisting of guitars, drums, and keyboard—plays an instrumental piece to signal that the service is about to begin. Their style is smartly contemporary, without being edgy. I assume Candy will appreciate their professional sound, while I'd prefer a bit more edge. We stand to sing for the opening set.

Afterward is a series of announcements, previewing the fall kickoff of various programs and reviewing the upcoming schedule. With all age groups present, we learn the average age at the church is twenty-seven. However, this isn't a church dominated by millennials, but more so one with a slew of kids and their Gen X parents.

They have a typical time for greeting. Though the people are nice as we shake hands, it's cursory, consisting of pleasant smiles and lacking connection. Aside from our family and hosts, this is the only time all morning we interact with anyone else. A clipboard moves down the row for us to leave our contact information. Candy enters our data, and I pass it to our friends.

For this denomination, this one is quite progressive, an outlier congregation. But based on my overall church experiences it's more middle-of-the-road. It's certainly not traditional, but it still retains hints of traditional elements.

Today is the final message of the sermon series, "Letters to the Angels," taken from Revelation 2 and 3. But before that, we're treated to a skit, a takeoff on Jimmy Fallon's thank-you notes routine, performed by their worship leader. It's done well, with relevant church humor, such as "Thank you, small group leaders, for doing work the staff doesn't want to do" and "Thank you, church volunteers, for essentially being unpaid employees." In handing the service to the minister, the worship leader jokes that he's thankful for only working one day a week.

The seventh letter, written to the angel of the church in Laodicea, is in Revelation 3:14–22. Whenever I've studied this passage, I've focused on the church being lukewarm and God's rejection of them as a result. Though the minister addresses this, his focus is on their smug self-complacency, which is also a pervasive issue in society today. We, like the church in Laodicea, need to "repent of being in control."

Their problem—as with today's culture, says the pastor— is their greed. "It's not all about me," he quips, decrying their self-focus. To their shame, they act as they do, relying on God's grace to get them into heaven. "He who has ears," concludes the pastor, as he quotes from the text, "let him hear."

When the service ends, most people head out, but we linger to talk with our family and friends. Though I thought the service was well attended, they say it was far below normal. I wonder about attendance at the second service.

I notice a Celtic cross on the side of the sanctuary and ask about its significance, but no one knows. As I recall, the circle that surrounds the intersection of the cross's two arms represents unity or eternity, two concepts I embrace: unity while on earth, followed by eternity in heaven.

Later, I talk with my son-in-law about the church. He likes it but wants something more contemporary, more like the church we went to before we moved. I agree with him and then wonder aloud if this might be the closest we'll find in this more traditional area.

Based on my experiences with this denomination,

they're contemporary compared to others in their denomination, an outlier. But they fall short of that compared to other churches.

The next day we talk about our experience when our son and daughter-in-law return home. They visited this church once and liked it but aren't sure why they never went back.

When I say, "No one else talked to us," they recall the same experience.

I tell Candy I could see myself going back.

She doesn't.

"I have no interest in returning."

"We'll see," I say. "This may be the closest match we'll find in the area."

She snorts. "I sure hope not."

Takeaway: Invite visitors to sit with you. And if you see someone you don't know, reach out to them. You might be the only person to talk to them.

THE RURAL CHURCH
COUNTRY FRESH

L ast Sunday we went to church with our daughter and son-in-law. This week we go with our son and his wife. However, we aren't going to their regular church. Instead, we'll visit one a couple miles from where they plan to move.

Part of an old denomination, the church recently changed their name, removing any hint of their affiliation, though the "About Us" section of their website still confirms their denominational connection. Their "Core Values and Beliefs" gives six descriptors and twenty-one articles of faith, taking 3,800 words to explain.

As I scan the list, my mind goes numb. *Can't Jesus be enough?*

Though this page is stodgy, the rest of the site has a warm, inviting feel that gives off an appealing vibe. On their home page, they ask, "Tired of boring faith and dull religion? What would it look like to live out a faith where you 'put it all on the line'?"

When they talk about a faith of adventure and risk, they draw me in. Who are they, a progressive church with a traditional heritage or a traditional church trying to appear more relevant? We'll soon find out.

On the drive there we're soon talking about what we might do the rest of the day, as if church is a prerequisite for what will follow. *We're losing focus.* "Who wants to pray for church?" Our son begins and I finish. My words aren't much different from what I typically ask, but the "Amen" possesses enhanced expectation. I share what I learned from their website, interspersed with speculation. We discuss the church for a while. We're primed for the experience by the time we arrive.

Right off a main street, they're easy to find. We pull into their parking lot to a bustle of activity. With two services, we arrive ten minutes early for the second one. We pick a space in a small parking lot in the front as we spot the drive to a larger one in back. With multiple buildings, this is a church facility and not what I expected for a rural country church in a small community.

We amble toward the door, and my normal pre-church visitor anxiety barely registers. Might I finally be used to visiting churches or is there confidence in numbers? I spot an open door on the side that reveals rows of chairs in what is likely the sanctuary, but we head to the main entrance.

Holding the door open with his back, a young towhead jiggles with antsy enthusiasm. He gives us a fervent greeting. "Welcome, y'all." Southern accents are rare in these parts, so I assume he's messing around but later realize his drawl is real. He hands out bulletins as our son and daughter-in-law walk by, dismayed when he realizes he only has one left for Candy and me.

"We'll share," Candy says. He directs the paper to me and then withdraws, again offering it to my wife. Apparently, his instructions are to give each person a bulletin, so that's what he intends to do. But Candy doesn't take it.

"I don't need one," I assure him as I walk past. He's still clinging to his last bulletin, perplexed that neither of us has taken it, when a man slips him another stack. Relieved that his dilemma is resolved, his eagerness returns, and we each take one.

Inside, no one else greets us. The crush of people causes us to weave our way between them as we move forward. An odor assaults me.

"Is it incense?" our daughter-in-law asks.

Candy thinks it might be, but I think it's just too much bad air freshener, attempting to cover up something even more offensive.

Our daughter-in-law leads the way but gives me a what-do-we-do glance.

I've done this enough that I have a ready answer. "If no one talks to us, we go in and find a place to sit."

Assured, she nods and presses toward the sanctuary. A young man, sporting an unobtrusive microphone, eyes us as we walk by. I consider introducing myself, but his silent demeanor tells me he's not interested. I avert my gaze and follow the rest of my family. We veer right and go up six rows.

Based on the building style, I suspect this part is about fifty years old. The cement block walls frame windows with rectangular panels of stained glass. They boast a rainbow of vibrant color on each side. Overhead, an understated cathedral ceiling provides an open feel.

The sanctuary is narrower and longer than most. It reminds me of many of the high churches we've visited. Though I don't know their denomination's tradition, I don't expect a high church experience.

Despite the constraints of the building, its contents are updated. First, there are no pews, but comfortable padded chairs. I estimate two hundred. There are no hymnals or Bibles, so I expect them to display everything we need on the monitors positioned around the room. One is centered in the front with four more flanking it, two per side. Subdued lighting gives a peaceful feel but doesn't produce enough light to read the bulletin comfortably.

As my eyes adjust, I'm relieved that my nose is now being spared, having left the odor in the narthex. Behind us a woman talks to her seatmate. She also has a southern accent, more pronounced than the boy at the door. I've heard only two people talk since we've arrived, and both had southern affectations. I wonder if we've stumbled into a refuge of southern expatriates. For many, this would conjure pleasant thoughts of charm and hospitality. For me—right or wrong—I associate southern accents at church with dogmatic evangelicalism. I brace myself to be assaulted by close-minded theology.

I have little time to contemplate this, however, as a man soon comes up to greet us. He's not sure if he's met us before and wonders if he should know our names. He's relieved when we tell him we're visiting.

He's one of the pastors here, and is an outgoing, friendly guy, a sharp contrast to the youth pastor who ignored us in the narthex. (In his defense, none of us fit his target demographic.) With introductions made, we share about ourselves, and he tells us about the church. By the time we wrap up our conversation, we feel embraced and informed.

Once again, I'm reminded how one person can make a difference in how a visitor perceives a church. I so appreciate him reaching out to us. While our daughter-in-law is amazed at his welcome, I'm dismayed that scores of people milling around left it up to their paid staff to welcome the newcomers. Still, having one person celebrate us is far better than everyone ignoring us, something Candy and I experienced too often at other churches.

By now, the worship team has gathered. Standing in a circle behind the monitor, they hold hands to pray. Their public example reminds me to do the same and hints that the service is about to start.

I check the clock as they begin to play. We're right on time, something I appreciate even though I suspect God is not as concerned with punctuality as I am. Our promptness is not important. Our worship is.

There are seven on the worship team: two guitars, bass guitar, keyboardist, and three vocalists. The keyboardist is also miked. There is no drummer or drum set. The pastor we met is the worship leader today. After the opening song, we have a greeting time. The people do well at greeting, but they don't excel at it—few churches do. Smiles and hand-shakes abound, but we don't connect. There's not enough time to talk. Perhaps the people know this and therefore don't try.

A video announcement plays, something we've only seen a few times at the largest of churches. A lengthy string of verbal announcements follows, ending with another video promoting the upcoming sermon series. Before singing resumes, we pray for the mission team heading off to Ecuador. After three more contemporary praise songs, the kids leave for their own activities. Before they go, I estimated seventy-five people present. Now that they're gone, I still estimate about seventy-five. Perhaps our initial number was closer to one hundred.

The lead pastor stands for the first time. Wearing jeans and a polo shirt, he holds an iPad for his sermon notes. There's no pulpit or lectern. This provides a casual feel, suggesting he'll teach us, not preach. Though his speech may retain the slightest trace of an accent, there's no hint of the narrow-minded dogma I feared.

He's nearing the end of a sermon series, "All In," about the life of Abraham. Today's message is "Let It Go," covering parts of Genesis 20 and 21. After sharing a personal story, he asks, "What's your number one obsession?"

He talks about sin and how to get rid of it, tying each of his three points back to Abraham's story, while weaving in other passages of Scripture. For persistent sin, we need to believe things can change. He reminds us of Genesis 18:14,

"Is anything too hard for God?" (TLB and MSG). This is my key takeaway of his message.

Later, he contrasts Abraham's two sons: Ishmael represents our old self, the old way—man's way. Isaac represents our new self, the new way—God's way. I wonder if he's stretching the text to make his point, but he cites Galatians 4:22–23 to support his assertion.

An unassuming man, he's not a charismatic orator, yet he's a most effective teacher. I have a page full of notes and much to contemplate. It's been too long since either one has happened.

He gives the closing prayer, complete with a time of commitment, but no altar call. Then we sing a closing song.

To end the service, the worship leader says, "Spend three minutes getting to know someone you don't know before talking with friends." I appreciate his directness about connecting with others. This should be standard at every church, but it seldom is. And I've never heard it explicitly stated. I wonder if the congregation will comply.

I need only ponder this for a moment when the couple in front of us turns around to talk. They invest much more time with us than three minutes, sharing life as we get to know each other. We form a connection. Others come up as well to introduce themselves. By the time we leave, we've made many connections and perhaps started friendships. I don't know how long the service was and how long we spent talking afterward, but we were there two hours, though it didn't seem that long.

At lunch, we discuss this church, sharing what we liked

and didn't like. Eventually I ask, "Do you see yourself going back?"

Three people say "Yes!" The fourth one isn't sure.

"Do you see yourself getting connected there?"

Again, three people say "Yes!" The fourth one doesn't answer.

The dissenter is my wife, the person who will pick which church she and I will attend. This means we have more churches to visit.

Takeaway: Look for visitors to talk to at your church. Seek your friends later.

THE KIND-OF-TRADITIONAL CHURCH

NOT SURE WHY

I t's time to leave for church, but our son isn't feeling well, and his wife will stay home with him. So, Candy and I make another last-minute change. It's 9:50 a.m., with not enough time to make it to any of the area's many 10 a.m. services. I scan my list of options (yes, we now have a list) and only five have later services. I pick a church that one of our future neighbors attends.

She's the first person we met in the neighborhood. We had an extended conversation about family and life, which led to talking about God and faith. When I asked what church her family attends, she rattled off the name, and I made a mental note to investigate. "But I'm not sure why we go there," she added with reservation. "I don't really like it; it's kind of traditional."

"How long have you gone there?"

"About fifteen years."

"That's a long time to go to a church you don't like."

"We have friends there," she explained. "It's comfortable."

"Yeah, community and connections are important, but still . . ."

"I guess it's easier to keep going than to change."

"Do your kids like it?"

She shrugged. "It's all they've ever known."

I want to probe some more, but I've already said too much to a person I just met. I remain silent and let her steer the conversation. She changes the subject.

So, we head to her church today, but I'm not sure why. Partly, I suppose, is out of respect for my new friend. I hope to see her and her family. Perhaps we can sit with them. But we should have planned for this, and with two morning services, our chances of seeing them are cut in half.

Another reason for going is to see if I agree with her assessment. Already I've decided I won't like the church, while at the same time I strive to remain open-minded. What a conundrum.

With an 11 a.m. service, we have plenty of time to arrive early—and we planned to—but by the time we get in the car, we don't have much of a cushion. I drive as Candy enters the address in our GPS.

I pray for the service and our time there.

The fall day is cool and the skies, gray. Windy, with intermittent rain, the gloomy weather matches my melan-choly mood. As we drive, the sun tries to break through the clouds to brighten my perspective. Unsuccessful, the clouds win, unleashing their torrent as we pull into the parking lot.

With no open spots by the door, I keep driving. That's when we spot another door on a newer part of their facility. This must be the main entrance, but there are no spots near it either. I keep driving. Though I expect to find spaces recently vacated by the first service crowd, I don't. *Will I ever find a place to park?* Eventually I do.

We brace ourselves against the wind and wet as we press toward the door. The facility is larger than I expected. The outside screams traditional. Inside, people mill about. I immediately notice two things: I'm decidedly underdressed, which doesn't surprise me, and we are in a throng of senior citizens, which does surprise me. I mentally recoil, over-whelmed by the glut of suits and gray hair, paired with dresses and blue-hued perms. Everyone looks a couple decades older than us. I feel out of place and am self-conscious. *Why are we here?*

People avoid making eye contact and may not even see us. Perhaps my blue jeans and tennis shoes are an affront to them, or maybe they're preoccupied with their own pre-service agenda. One man is the exception, not only making eye contact but smiling too. He extends his hand and welcomes me. I reciprocate and am about to share my name when I realize he's not ready for further interaction. We press toward the sanctuary.

The traditional vibe escalates as we weave our way, invisible, among the mass of people. "Aren't there any bulletins?" asks my wife. "You'd think a church like this would have bulletins." I agree but don't see any either.

Finally, she spots a man holding a stack of papers. She approaches him and asks. He hands her one. Pleased, she rejoins me, and we sit in the second of four sections, about a third of the way forward.

The bulletin says they have a conference this weekend, with a guest speaker today. Inwardly I sigh. We came to experience their normal service, not an atypical one.

The bulletin also reports last week's statistics. The attendance was 507, evenly split between the two services. Sixty percent of those folks also went to Sunday school between the morning services. For their evening service, 217 people showed up.

Their general fund, comprising 63 percent of their budget, is lagging their year-to-date target by a few percentage points. They also have a building fund, at 19 percent of their goal, which is slightly ahead of where they hoped to be.

Most encouraging, however, is their missions fund. I'm impressed they have one and that it's 17 percent of their total budget. Even more remarkable, their year-to-date missions contributions are 27 percent ahead of their goal. This is a giving church, and I applaud their desire to support outreach efforts. They also have off-budget items for benevolence and debt-retirement.

I suspect the sanctuary seats about four or five hundred. It will end up being about 75 percent full. Though I see a handful of younger families and a few mid-lifers, most are in their senior citizen years. I question the wisdom of expanding their facility when their numbers will decrease through attrition over the next ten years.

A man comes up and introduces himself. "Are you

visiting today?" He's wearing a wireless ear mic, so I assume he's the pastor.

"Yes, we are." He's only the second person to talk to me and the first who said more than "Hi." I want to make the most of our interaction.

"Is this your first time here?" he asks, even though he knows the answer.

Candy and I both smile, nodding our enthusiasm. "Yes, it is!"

"Great! I'm glad you're here today. Did you receive our welcome gift when you came in?"

I want to tell him no one even talked to us. Instead, I shake my head.

"Well, be sure to get it on the way out." But he doesn't tell us where.

If I'm to do as he says, I need more details. "Okay," I say with a lack of conviction. The obvious solution, the visitor-friendly approach, would be for him to go get a welcome gift and give it to us.

Satisfied with my response, he smiles broadly. "You're in for a real treat today! We have a special guest speaker."

"So we won't get to hear you, then?"

"Oh, no. I'm not the teaching pastor. I'm the visitation pastor. You'll see me up front a little today but not much. Our teaching pastor is really good. Our guest speaker is even better. It will be a great service." As we talk, he's also distracted by someone vying for his attention. Finally, he excuses himself to address this pressing need. I expect he'll return to finish our conversation, but he moves on to other people, so I return to checking out the sanctuary.

Even with a baby grand piano and an area for a large choir, the huge stage provides ample space. Their motto, projected overhead, reads "Living His Truth, Loving His People, Sharing His Message." Arrayed in a circle, I'm not sure which element comes first. Maybe it doesn't matter. Later I check their website for clarity, but it gives a different motto: "Changing Lives for Eternity."

The service opens with a welcome and announcements. Then there's time for "personal, private prayer." But by the time I note those words in my journal, the personal, private prayer time is over, and the leader gives the opening prayer.

Though there was an organ prelude, we sing with piano accompaniment. After two hymns, there's a congregational prayer, which morphs into the offertory prayer. With the "Amen," the ushers pass the offering plates while the organ plays "Take My Life and Let It Be." Then we sing a third song.

Our guest speaker is an apologetics preacher. I groan to myself. Apologetics, which I've always thought was a strange name, is a reasoned, systematic defense of a theological position. Though the older crowd will delight in his teaching, I will not. I've experienced apologetics as close-minded, lacking in grace and abounding with critical conviction. Speakers leave no room for disagreement, presenting their opinions as fact and expecting everyone to agree with them. Dissenters are surely heretics.

Though apologetics predates the modern era, I perceive it, and its cousin, systematic theology, primarily as constructs of the modern era, which fueled their popularity. However, if God deemed a holistic, theological treatise as important, he'd have surely detailed it in the Bible—and Paul would have been the person to write it. He did not—or at least I've not found it yet.

Ironically, the speaker says he's focused on today's youth. Does he know they're primarily postmodern thinkers? I doubt apologetics holds much interest for them and may even reinforce their disillusionment with Christianity and the institutional church. This doesn't matter too much since few youth are present. Instead, their modern-thinking grandparents are here, and they will enjoy his teaching and clamor for more.

The title of his message is "Becoming Bold." After some introductory remarks, he shares a surprising statistic: "There are 400,000 churches in the US and only 6,000 first-run movie theaters." He pauses for effect and repeats it a second time. Then he adds, "But we've lost our influence. We're hardly even noticeable."

Though this may not be a fair comparison, it's a sobering one. It's also the most interesting thing he says his entire message and the last thing I write. Eventually I close my notebook.

The conference's intent is to give us a reason for hope, but by the end of the message, I feel only despair. I heard nothing of hope. I felt no love. But I do feel alienated. This is not because I disagreed with the speaker's message, but because his narrow interpretation left no room for divergent views. He single-handedly became the poster child of everything I see wrong with narrow-minded, modern-thinking preachers. I can't wait to leave.

Even though my spirit is seething, I still hope for some

post-service interaction, to experience a bit of Christian community. Though we linger, no one approaches us, and I can't catch anyone's eye, despite sometimes holding my gaze long enough to border on staring.

We walk slowly. I wonder if someone will offer us the promised welcome gift, while not caring if they do. No one does.

By now we're out of the sanctuary and halfway to the exit. My pulse quickens as my soul's angst, a spiritual indignation, threatens to overflow. A primal instinct to flee bubbles up inside me. "I've got to get out of here," I hiss out of the corner of my mouth. I don't know if my wife hears me, but as the pressure on my chest builds, I stride toward the door with intention.

Even so, I make one last, futile attempt at eye contact with an older man as I push through the double doors to make my escape. He doesn't even glance at me. Perhaps it's for the best.

Now free, I gulp fresh air. Though the hard rain has stopped, it's still misting. I'm glad for this moisture hitting my face, for it will mask my tears that threaten to erupt. I plaster on a false smile as I stride toward the car. Once inside I finally feel safe. Now I can breathe again. I take a deep, cleansing breath.

I want to vent, but know that's a bad idea, because I could lose the last bit of control I have over the pent-up emotion amassing inside me. With a calm, even voice, I finally seek my bride's opinion. "So, what did you think?"

My modern-thinking wife really liked the message, as I

knew she would. Eventually she answers my underlying but unasked question. "But I don't want to go back."

I'm so relieved.

Takeaway: If you want to cater to your members, give them what they want. If you want to attract new people, give them what they need—even if it makes some members upset.

THE CHURCH WITH MUCH TO OFFER
INTRIGUING POSSIBILITIES

The neighbor who goes to *The Kind-of-Traditional Church* also mentioned this one. "All the rest of the neighbors go there," she said. "It's more contemporary." That's where we're headed today, all the while questioning how many of our future neighbors actually go there.

The facility is larger than I expect and the parking lot, huge. With minimal congestion, it's easy to find an open spot. The main entrance is obvious, and we walk toward it, along with many others who converge there from their parking spaces. Several people stand outside to greet arrivals. They're friendly in excess, but there's no effort at anything more than to flash a broad smile and offer a hearty handshake. Their apparent intent is to keep us moving forward, funneling us indoors.

Among the bustle of activity inside, many people pause to share an inviting smile and state their welcome, often accompanied with a handshake. But the interaction stops at that point as they hustle off to something else. Though the contact lacks depth, it's encouraging they noticed us at all, far different from our experience at the last church.

I scan the lobby—quickly, to not look pathetically lost—hoping to spot the welcome center. Seeing nothing, and no one who beckons us, we mill forward toward the sanctuary, which is actually a smartly accessorized gymnasium. It reminds Candy of "Church #45: Another Doubleheader" in *52 Churches*: a full-sized gym with a large stage on the side, hundreds of padded chairs, and plenty of room to move about. She's right, and I nod my agreement.

She heads to the center aisle and moves forward with intention. Fearful she wants to sit too far toward the front for my wellbeing, I halt her onward movement. "This is far enough." I turn into the back row of the front section, move in a few seats, and sit. To my relief she joins me.

I calculate the room has eight hundred chairs and estimate about two hundred people present. By the time they dismiss the children for their own activities, I suspect the crowd has swelled to 350.

A large screen over the ample stage displays a countdown timer until the service begins. Two larger screens flank it, repeating the same information. As the worship team assembles onstage, a fourth screen behind us cues them on what the congregation sees. At T-minus three minutes, they begin playing.

The worship team is so large that I count three times to confirm they number fourteen. The musicians are arrayed in an arc: French horn, trombone, baby grand piano, drum kit, keyboard, bass guitar, and two electric guitars. In front of them stand six vocalists, including the song leader on acoustic guitar.

As a prelude, they sing softly. Their contemporary sound is practiced but with no hint of an edge or excess energy. A rock concert it is not. Even though the words for this first song appear on the screens, most people don't join in, instead continuing to talk.

At T-minus two seconds, the song ends, and a video announcement plays, followed by a string of verbal messages from a man who gives only his first name. Next week is infant dedication, followed in a few weeks by adult baptisms. He jokes about them providing donuts as an incentive for people to go to the first service instead of the fuller second one. Then he segues into an opening prayer, which precedes the offering. A concluding song serves to transition us to the message.

Another man stands, but he doesn't give his name. With too many pastors who are quick to drop their title—and even their advanced degree—at every opportunity, I appreciate he doesn't. He has either the humility or self-confidence to skip this, but I wish to at least know his first name.

His message is from the book of Nehemiah, "a case study in leadership." Focusing on select verses in chapter two, he talks about the city walls being in shambles, but the people accept this as reality and do nothing to repair them. "Many churches ignore their problems," he says. To highlight this, he shows a video clip titled, "It's not about the nail."

I've seen this before, and I delight in watching it again,

while my bride groans at the unexpected reveal midway through. "Never allow fairness to determine our receptiveness to being obedient to God," he reminds us. Under Nehemiah's leadership, the people rebuild the wall in only fifty-two days.

He then moves to two other verses, Philippians 2:5 and Acts 2:42, focusing on them for the rest of his message. He concludes by hinting at why churches are dying, which parallels why the city wall of Nehemiah's day remained broken. The solution to dying churches is adopting the same attitude as the people did under Nehemiah's leadership: "They were willing to give up their personal agendas in order to be obedient to God."

I have a page of notes and jotted down several pithy one-liners, but despite all this, I can't follow the flow of his message and connect the dots. Still, he gave me much to consider. After concluding his sermon, he prays we would "know what we stand for; not what we stand against." We'll do well to follow his advice.

As we leave the gym, ushers hand out key tags with the message's two *key* verses. "Your attitude should be the same as that of Christ Jesus. Philippians 2:5" is on one side. The other proclaims, "They devoted themselves to the apostles' teaching and to the fellowship, to the breaking of bread and to prayer. Acts 2:42." (They don't list the version, but I later find both in the NIV, 1996 version.)

I'm puzzled. Why did they give us key tags with these two verses? How do they tie in with the first part of the message and the conclusion? What are we supposed to do with them?

Returning to the lobby, we make our way to the information table to pick up a free book for first-time visitors. They offer us three to consider. I've read two of them, so I opt for the third. Though the title doesn't interest me, and I'm not sure I'll read it, I don't see a graceful way to decline. We talk with the two people there for a few minutes. Despite the ample number of folks who welcomed us, or invited us back, they are the only two to ask our names or share theirs.

Outside stand the minister and another man, greeting people as they arrive for the second service and saying goodbye to those leaving the first. Just as at our arrival, their focus is on interacting with as many as possible but doing so quickly. I abandon my hope to talk with the pastor. Even though no one else is nearby vying for his attention right now, his gaze is far away.

On the drive home, we discuss our experience. Candy calls the music "safe," and I agree. She didn't like the message. While I did, it's not so much because I followed it, but because of a few thought-provoking insights.

"They were friendly," she adds with a hopeful tone.

"Yes, but it was all superficial," I counter. "We didn't have any meaningful conversations and didn't make any connections."

She nods. "Do you think any of our new neighbors go there?"

"I didn't recognize anyone."

On the surface, this church has a lot going for it and much to offer with their contemporary music, intriguing message, larger size, newer building, and friendly people.

But I fear it would require much effort and take a long time to make meaningful connections.

We could come back sometime, perhaps for their second service, but I doubt we will.

Takeaway: Know what you stand for, not what you stand against.

THE CHURCH WITH THE FUNDAMENTAL VIBE
PEOPLE MAKE THE DIFFERENCE

All day Saturday I fight the threat of a cold, applying equal parts prayer and pills to conquer it. What I need is sleep—desperately. By Sunday morning, Candy's not surprised when I tell her I'm staying home.

"Fine, I'll go myself." She's not defiant, just decisive. She's an independent spirit. I appreciate her confidence to go alone and without complaint.

Relieved at her acceptance of my decision to stay home, I nod in agreement as I close my eyes. Sleep overtakes me.

The church she picked is an independent congregation with an evangelical past and fundamental vibe. She knows two couples who attend there, former coworkers whose company she enjoys and whose faith walk she respects. I've met them briefly over the years. They're good folks.

During the week we talked about visiting this church. While I had a different destination in mind—another megachurch—Candy lobbied for this one. By the time Saturday rolled around, I didn't much care, giving my assent because it was too hard to discuss.

I don't hear her leave, and the next thing I know she's back.

Though still needing rest, my two-hour nap offered some improvement.

"What was it like?"

She responds, but I struggle to focus and don't remember what she said.

Later, I ask again. She liked the church but mostly talks about seeing her friends. I wish I'd felt good enough to go, but I know that would've been a mistake. Today I needed rest much more than I needed community.

A third time, I question her further. It reminds her of a church we attended twenty years ago. She means this in a favorable way, but what I hear is this church is at least a decade out of date.

"I'd like you to go with me sometime," she says, "but I don't think you'll like it."

My expectation sinks. I want to groan, but that would take too much effort. Confused, I nod to show I heard. Then I fall asleep again.

I'm sure she'll take me there sometime. Unfortunately, she did little to sell me on it.

Takeaway: If you're enthusiastic about your church or your faith, be sure to communicate it and not leave people wondering.

THE NONCONVENTIONAL CHURCH
LOCKED OUT

We head for a church that meets in an office complex, using space provided by an adoption agency. A former coworker of Candy's is the teaching elder there. Another of her friends recently started attending. The thought of knowing someone at church is a powerful pull.

Lacking a website, they do have a Facebook page. However, aside from oodles of photos and a few dated reviews, there's only one other thing I can learn about them. However, it's monumental. The words quicken my heart. A simple but laden question asks, "What does a church look like when you drop all the programs, masks, facades, and actually learn to love one another in participation of the Way of Christ?"

Sloppy writing aside, this is definitely a church I want to check out. They may be the kindred spirits I seek. Dare I hope they'll live up to the implied promise of their spiritually provocative statement?

An early winter snow makes traveling slippery. Wet feathery flakes of white threaten to cover the road, obscuring our visibility. I wonder if we should even be out driving. Through a mix of partial information and assumptions, we get lost, stumbling on the building by accident once we've given up any hope of finding it. We pull into the parking lot six minutes late.

Amid multiple buildings, with a slew of tenants, we spot the adoption agency, but their door is locked. An adjacent entry marked "employee entrance" is locked too. After wandering around in the cold, wet snow, we finally spot a third entrance in another building that also lists their name. This one, with its double doors, is more promising, but it is likewise shut tight.

Fighting off the fluffy dampness of the falling snow, we walk around the complex, looking for hints of where to go or how to get in. Some sections of the walks are shoveled; most are not. Random footprints in the snow reveal recent traffic, but they don't converge on a common entrance or even hint at a way inside. Frustrated, we get back in our car and drive around the facility, looking for their church sign or another entrance to try. When this yields no new clues, we return to the parking lot.

There are other cars there, so we know people are present. Having given up, I remain in the car. Candy gets out and presses her ear against the glass in the double doors and hears music emanating from deep inside. She rattles the doors, and even pounds, but garners no response. After waiting in exasperation, she repeats her efforts, this time with more fervor and increased ire.

She returns to the car, fuming. Now twenty-five minutes after the start of their service, my impulse is flight, while hers is to fight. At an impasse and not knowing what else to do, we drive home in silence, wondering how something so simple could go so wrong.

Though we encountered locked doors at some churches, we eventually found one that was open. This time we did not.

Later that day, my wife vents to the teaching elder in a private Facebook message. He apologizes but doesn't explain the locked doors. He provides a vague description of which entrance we should have used, but if we understand correctly, we tried it.

We'll attempt to visit them again, arriving early so we can be sure to get inside. This congregation claims to have a different approach to doing church, and I must learn more. But I'm not sure if I can work past my frustration of being locked out in the cold while the faithful gathered in the warmth inside. I may have already decided against this church, and I haven't even been to their service.

Takeaway: Make sure visitors know where your church is located and what entrance to use.

A SECOND CHANCE TO MAKE A
FIRST IMPRESSION

TRYING AGAIN

Two weeks later we head back to *The Nonconventional Church*. The implication that this congregation does church in a different way intrigues me. However, I'm still harboring hurt from them effectively excluding us from their gathering on our first attempt to visit.

With two weeks to stew about this, I'm still peeved when we get in the car on Sunday morning. I don't want to pray for a good attitude. I don't want to pray for the church service we hope to encounter. Praying about this, however—I realize too late—is what I should have been doing for the past fourteen days.

I ask Candy to pray. She declines. I grunt out a petition to the Almighty using phrases oft repeated when we head for church: "May we receive what you would have us to receive. May we give to others what you would have us to give. And may we worship you today in spirit and in truth."

Then I add a begrudging afterthought. "Oh, and give me a good attitude. Yeah. Amen."

Feeling guilty over my halfhearted prayer, I suspect God isn't pleased either. I have little hope my pitiful plea, one offered more out of obligation than expectation, will gain much traction with the godhead. I sigh.

Once again Candy had some last-minute communication with her friend at this church. Though their Facebook page says 9:30, he assures her it starts at 10 a.m. Today he tells us to go through the door of a travel agency and not the adoption service. That would have been helpful information last time. At least today we know where the building is. We also leave early to give us extra time. We hope to time our arrival with other attendees and follow them inside. Unfortunately, Candy's friend will not be there to look for us. He had a bad encounter with a halibut at dinner last night and is home recovering from food poisoning.

We arrive about ten minutes early, not as early as Candy wanted. Again, there are cars in the parking lot, but we see no people. We sit for a while, waiting for others to arrive. They don't. We scan the building, searching for the name of the travel agency. We don't see it.

However, I spot a different travel agency. "Do you think he gave us the wrong name?" Candy's not sure, but I think he did. We double-check all the other signs. With no other travel agencies, I assume he misspoke.

We get out of the car and head in that direction. Only when we're almost to the door do we spot a small, ground-level sign for the church. While most helpful to us now, we had to get out of our car to see it. We would've never noticed it from the parking lot.

Inside, to our right, is the inner door to the travel agency. It's shut and the lights inside are off. To the left is a glow, emanating from a stairwell around the corner. We head toward the light. Though wide, the stairway is otherwise unimpressive: dirty and well worn. At the bottom we see new construction injected into an old facility. Though the hallway is lit in both directions, we hear people to our left. We head toward the murmuring.

We approach a hall with trepidation. However, before we make it to the doors, a woman I recently met while volunteering looks up in surprise to see us. She walks to us with intention, offering a hearty greeting. I'm pleased to see someone I know in this new area where I know so few.

As we talk, several of Candy's friends spot her and come up to welcome us. None of them expected her, but all are pleased we're visiting. As we talk, we learn more about their situation.

First, this church is about thirty years old and not the startup I assumed. My friend was one of the founding members. The fact that they meet in rented space after three decades encourages me, reinforcing their claim they're committed to break from church conventions. Without owning a building, they're free from the financial burden it entails. The owner of the facility is indeed the adoption agency, so our initial information was correct, though misleading. The basement recently flooded and is undergoing repairs. It will take a couple more weeks to finish.

The reason no people arrived with us is that they all

came at 9 a.m. for Sunday school, with classes for all ages. Each class covers the same topic but with age-appropriate content. I appreciate this twist, as it allows families to encounter the same curriculum but at accessible levels, providing the opportunity for further discussion at home. At the same time, I wish they'd broken from the habit of Sunday school, as its original intent—to teach illiterate people how to read—no longer applies. Yet the expectation to provide Sunday school lives on.

A bit overwhelmed by all the attention, I sit down to wait for the service to start. I review the names of people I've met, jotting them in my notebook on the page reserved for today's experience. I suspect I'll see these folks again, so I work to remember names.

Aside from being in a meeting space in the basement of an office building, the room is configured as expected for a church service. About seventy chairs, set in three sections, are arced to face a podium centered in the front. The worship team assembles to the right of the lectern. An impressive drum kit sits in the other corner. Housed in a Plexiglas enclosure, it seems even grander. Couches fill the space behind us, with the soundboard in the back corner.

The service opens with a family reading three Scripture selections and lighting the first Advent candle. They give way to the worship team of nine, a mixture of teens and adults, sporting an eclectic mix of instruments: violin, saxophone, drums, keyboard, guitar, and bass guitar. The song leader stands behind the podium, directing us with his strong, soothing voice as his arms sway to keep time. Two female backup vocalists stand between him and the instrumentalists. We sing for about thirty minutes, mostly Christmas songs, with a lively crowd-pleaser in the middle. Part way through the song set is the offering. People walk forward to present their donations, while the rest of us sing. Throughout the singing, many people raise their arms in an act of physical worship.

Because of the flood, there is no children's church today, and they expect a few more weeks before repairs are complete. The kids, who are many, remain with us for the message. I estimate fifty people present, including the worship team. It's a comfortable-sized gathering, with all age groups, though a slight majority are families with younger kids. There also appear to be a few three-generation family units sitting together. I enjoy seeing kids migrate to their grandparents' laps as the service progresses.

With their teaching elder at home recovering from his food poisoning, another member fills in to give today's lesson. He's comfortable in front of the group, and though he's had little time to prepare, he ably fills in, speaking for an hour. "Advent," he says, "is a time of waiting." We wait with hope, in anticipation, and full of excitement. Later he expounds on our time of waiting: "We don't have what God wants to give us because we didn't cry out for it." He cites a verse in Psalms, but I must have written it down wrong. Later I find nine verses in Psalms with the phrase "cry out," and I'm not sure which one he cited. Still, his question of "What are we crying out for?" is a convicting one.

The last segment of the service is a time of prayer, with our leader opening it and members who take turns praying. Some come forward and use the mic, while others pray from where they sit—both adults and children. They direct their words to God and not to impress others or to promote an agenda, which I've seen too often in group prayer. Unfortunately, during the periods of silence between the petitions, my mind drifts. *What time is it? How much longer will this last? What's for lunch?*

Our leader offers a concluding prayer, and the service is over, but no one leaves.

Most of the people we talked to earlier come up again to thank us for visiting and invite us back. A few people mention the need for signs to guide visitors to the correct door. Apparently, our inability to get inside two weeks ago has circulated. While no one mentions our dilemma directly or apologizes, they do acknowledge they're working to address this problem.

My friend gives me a copy of *The Story*, which is the basis for their Sunday school lessons. I feel guilty in accepting the gift, but it would be rude to decline. I do, however, appreciate her gesture and sincerely thank her.

Some kids gather around a table in back, playing an intense game of cards. I smile. According to my wife's fundamental upbringing, these "devil cards" are explicitly forbidden. It would be sacrilegious to play with them at church. Yet here they are.

Despite all the people who welcome us, it only comes from those our age. None of the younger adults talk to us. While there may be many legitimate reasons for this— ranging from other people for them to greet, the reality we were already welcomed well, or of pressing issues with their children—I feel slighted.

Too many churches unofficially, yet effectively, segregate by age. Though it's natural for people to gravitate toward those most like them—especially those their age—we have more to gain by interacting with people of different ages, at different life stages. This is the hallmark of a truly multigenerational church, as this church hints at being.

Eventually we head out, the first to do so. I don't know how long the others will linger in community. Though I long to do so, too, I don't know anyone well enough for an in-depth conversation, and I have exhausted all my socially polite talk.

On our way home, we discuss our experience. Without asking her, I know Candy likes the church and wants to go back. While a return visit is in order, I don't share her level of enthusiasm. Though they're high on my list, they're top on my bride's.

My fear is she's already decided where she wants to go, while I'm not so sure. Regardless, I know we'll one day revisit this church.

Takeaway: As far as Christian community is concerned, it's what happens after the service that has the most impact.

EXPERIENCING THE CHURCH WITH THE FUNDAMENTAL VIBE

CANDY IS RIGHT

Today Candy makes a return trip to *The Church with the Fundamental Vibe*, this time with me in tow. The first time she went, I stayed home sick. She didn't tell me much about the service, but she enjoyed reconnecting with friends. She also predicted I wouldn't like it, so I'm not sure why we're going back. I pray for a good attitude and an open mind.

It's the Sunday between Christmas and New Year's. The weather is unseasonably warm, with no snow on the ground and no clouds in the sky. The drive is pleasant and quick. Flanking the large facility is ample parking. I expected something smaller.

As we hang up our coats, a woman talks with Candy. I assume they know each other. Wanting to be supportive, I join in. However, they don't know each other.

Despite that, our new acquaintance concisely shares a lot of helpful information. "Normally we have a Bible study hour after the church service but not today because of the holidays." She pauses and then smiles over what she's about to share next. "And normally we have a Sunday evening service but not today because of the holidays."

I smile. "Taking a break?"

"We want to focus on family time. Some people are traveling, and others have family visiting." They're between senior pastors and their interim pastor will speak today. "He's really good." Then she adds, "We'd like him to become our regular pastor, but he's not interested."

Not having anything to add, I nod to show I'm listening and encourage her to share more.

"It's been about a year so far and we expect it to take another year," she adds. "But while we wait, we're in good hands." She beams.

"I really appreciate knowing all this. Thanks so much for telling us."

She points us to the sanctuary and then excuses herself. Never has someone shared so much helpful information about their church before the service. I feel informed and not so apprehensive over what awaits me.

Candy guides me into the sanctuary, a huge square room of newer construction. It boasts a minimalist vibe but with smatterings of elegant furnishings scattered about. She heads to the section on the far left. Last time her friends sat in this area, and she expects to find them here again. Along the way, she surprises another person as she walks by. "Candy? Candy, is that you?"

I stop and nod to the stranger. "Yes, that's Candy." I wait for my wife to realize I'm no longer following her and to come back. She does and reconnects with yet another former coworker. This friend, we learn, lives a couple miles from us. Today she is running sound and excuses herself to make last-minute preparations.

Candy does indeed find two of her friends, sitting right where she expected. They make room for us to sit with them. Settling in, I glance at the bulletin, a trifold affair, more attractive than most and packed with useful information. However, it's not until we get home that I spot the part about stopping by the visitor center and staying afterward for the Visitor's Coffee.

I miss reading this in the bulletin because the stage distracts me. At first glance it gives a pleasant vibe, but it's an overdone arrangement that visually assaults me. Do we really need faux trees on the platform?

Interspersed among the staging, the worship team prepares for the service. The worship leader plays a baby grand piano, and then there's a violin, with a conga drum next to it but pushed into the background. Also part of this eclectic group is a guitar, harp, and keyboard, with the lead vocalist front and center. I suspect they think the service is contemporary—and thirty years ago it was—but today it's merely safe, skewing toward traditional.

What captures my attention is the girl on the conga. Accomplished, I'm sure she's holding back to match the rest of the group. Occasionally the hint of a smile threatens to overtake her already pleasant face. I sense she's itching to cut loose and play her heart out. Though I'm sure that would please God, the rest of the congregation might not be so appreciative.

I estimate the sanctuary seats 1,200, and it's mostly full by the time the service starts. I try to sing along, but my efforts fall flat. The words elude their formation on my lips. I'd rather watch the conga girl and her mesmerizing playing. Her demeanor exudes peace as her inviting rhythm draws me to God. Is it possible to worship God vicariously through the musical skill of another? I think I can. I hope I am. If not, God will be disappointed today with my worship of him.

Failing to engage in anything other than the drum player, everything else blurs. There's more singing, a prayer or two, some announcements, and a greeting time, but the details escape me. I want to connect, both with God and with others, but I'm mired in the routine of church boredom. Though Candy's prediction of my reaction is proving correct, I really hoped she would've been wrong.

We segue into the sermon. Part four of a four-part series on "Christmas Names for Jesus," today the focus is on the "Prince of Peace," courtesy of Isaiah 9:6. I once memorized this passage for a church Christmas play when I was in middle school. Though the minister isn't reading from the King James Version, that's the version I learned for the program and those are the words that resound in my head now.

Memories of that performance resurface: My parents' pleasure over my flawless recitation—after weeks of practice. My pride in turning an ordinary bath towel into a reasonable representation of shepherd head garb, inspired by Linus in "A Charlie Brown Christmas." Fun hanging out with my church friends. And a random classmate who unexpectedly showed up and mocked my involvement in something so hokey. Fortunately, he forgot about it by the time we returned to school, so I was spared further embarrassment.

Oh yeah, Prince of Peace. I push aside these memories and try to focus on the words of the preacher. He unpacks the word *peace* as I scribble key phrases in my notebook. Jumping to Luke 2:14, ". . . and on earth peace . . . ." He then follows with a dozen or more New Testament verses about *peace.* Easy to listen to, he moves effortlessly from one verse to the next, from one thought to another. After his resurrection, Jesus gives his disciples peace (John 20:19, 21, and 26).

The end of his message doubles as the benediction: "Peace be with you through Jesus."

The daughter of Candy's friends, whom we sat with, wasn't feeling well and left midway through the message. By the end of the service, the entire family is gone so we can't talk with them. The others sitting near us are also unavailable, though we do talk with her friend who ran sound, which is good.

Later, as I wait for Candy outside the women's restroom, a lady comes up who recognizes me. What a surprise. In this area, my bride often runs into people who know her, but this is only the second time it's happened to me. The woman is on staff at the church, and she knows me from a writers' conference where I spoke. We have a warm conversation. It's nice to be known and welcomed.

On the drive home, I process my thoughts aloud about the preacher and his message. "He's a gifted speaker:

polished, articulate, and accomplished." Candy nods in agreement. "He's comfortable in front of a group and most knowledgeable about the Bible. He's easy to listen to . . . and I was completely bored."

"Yeah, I didn't think you'd like it."

She was right.

Takeaway: If your church is still doing what you did thirty years ago, what should change?

THE STRENGTHS AND WEAKNESSES OF BIG

RETURNING TO THE MEGACHURCH

W e arrived late the first time we visited *The Megachurch*. Our tardy arrival seriously skewed my experience that day. I knew we'd need to make a return visit. Today we do.

We plan to leave early, but it doesn't work out. Even so, we leave early enough to arrive fifteen minutes before the service starts. We park in about the same area as last time, and this time we know which direction to head. Our first visit was on a pleasant fall day, with a gentle sun and warm breeze. Today is the middle of winter. Though it's not snowing, the temperatures hover in the mid-twenties, and the biting wind attacks us with fervor. My winter coat fails to protect me. I stride toward the door with purpose.

Glad to be inside, I head straight to the "first-time visitors" pavilion. Several people stand ready to welcome us. I flash my best smile. "Hi!"

"Is this your first time here?"

Oh no, busted! "We visited once before," I try to explain, "but got here late and . . ." I shake my head at the memory and try to stifle a shudder. I search for more words to justify our audacity at approaching the "first-time visitors" table even though we aren't first timers.

The lady smiles and offers reassurance. "Who would like to fill out the visitors' card?"

"The person whose handwriting we can read," I say, gesturing to Candy. She always fills out the information card.

The woman hands me a coffee mug and offers a second so "you can both have one."

I shake my head. "I don't drink coffee." I suspect I sound rude, but we don't need any more church coffee cups. The woman accepts this and doesn't show she took offense. I realize that if a person ever needed coffee cups, they could start visiting churches and would quickly amass a cupboard full, albeit mismatched.

Then she hands me a "Get Connected" pamphlet, a 40-page booklet with the subtitle "Grow, Connect, Impact." Many churches use these words or others like them. Theologically I embrace the idea, but execution is the key. "This explains all about our church," she gushes. "We're a big church, so small groups are important to us. We encourage everyone to be in one. That's the best way to get connected."

I nod, confirming the importance of a small group and the community it can offer.

"I really encourage you to visit the small group table."

She points to an area behind me. "They can find a group in your area that's a good match for you."

I nod again, wanting to tell her how much I agree and how badly I want to be in an intentional spiritual community, one focused on mutual support and encouragement, one where we can help each other on our faith journeys. But before I can marshal the words, she continues.

"You can go there now or visit them after the service."

"Okay." I'm tempted to. Yet I also know that if the group is all I hope it to be, I'd see no need to attend church on Sunday. *Could I be in one of their small groups and not go to their church?* Not that anyone would know, with their two services and thousands of people. Yet it wouldn't feel right.

She hands me another packet, this one bearing a CD to explain the history of their church. Interested in learning more, I'm happy to accept it.

By this time Candy has completed the information card. She cradles her new coffee cup, and we head to the sanctuary. This time we enter a different door. We also sit in a different section, mindful of how the continuous movement of the boom cameras throughout the entire service distracted me.

By the time we select our seats, the countdown timer is at 5:00. I'm surprised at how few people there are. Actually, there are hundreds, but with more empty seats than occupied ones, the space looks empty. With one minute left, the lights dim to hint that the service is about to begin. The crowd is still sparse.

When the counter hits zero, the band starts. Some

people join in, but not many. The song isn't familiar to us. I wonder if it's new to everyone. I'm reminded again about how much there is to distract me. The large screens overhead, the boom cameras, the camera operators roving the stage with their handhelds, the praise choir swaying with the music, the dozen or more musicians and singers on the worship team—and the steady stream of people flowing into the sanctuary.

I don't know the second song or the third, but I mouth some of the words, which is easier on the choruses. Some lyrics hit me as significant, but I can't focus on them, since I'm trying to move my lips while trying to ignore all the surrounding distractions. Even though we are sitting halfway toward the front, we're still too far back to see much detail of the people on stage. It feels more like a concert than a church service. I wonder if a concert vibe is their intent.

The order unfolds the same as before. The prayer team comes forward and people wanting prayer follow. There's the briefest of greeting times. By now, the main floor is mostly full, but from what I can see, the balcony is mostly empty. The attendance appears the same as at our first visit. Then the pastor gives a brief teaching on giving, from Matthew 6:20, before they take the offering.

We sing another song and watch a video about small groups. Sometimes they say "small groups" and other times they use "life groups." (Their literature uses *life groups*, but their website uses both terms.) The phrases mean different things to me, with *small groups* being more transient and *life groups* being long term.

The announcement ends with "sign up today; groups start next week." This suggests they run small groups in terms, with periodic reshuffling. That way if you end up in a group you don't like, it won't last long. However, there may not be enough time for a group to really gel and become all it can. With these concerns, the pull of being in one of their small groups diminishes.

Today they have a guest speaker, a missionary from the other side of the world. His English is perfect and his diction, flawless, yet it seems his words are colored by the culture he ministers to. Though his intent is clear, his occasionally odd phrasing disrupts my concentration.

Reading from the KJV (last time the minister used the NKJV), he teaches from Paul's letter to the Philippians. He promises we'll "learn something from the Bible we've never heard before." It's an audacious claim. I'm skeptical. Though he unveils historical context that's new to me, he doesn't teach me anything new about the contents of the Bible itself—or maybe I missed it.

Then midway through the message, he switches to a lengthy illustration about evolving technology, obsolescence, and the need to adapt to changing conditions. Then, just as abruptly, he takes us back to Philippians. I see no connection between his illustration and the lesson on joy from Philippians. This reminds me of Luke 19:12–26, which seems to be a mash-up of two unrelated parables, with one shoved inside the other.

To conclude, he launches into an altar call of sorts, leading the entire congregation in a prayer of salvation. I always bristle at this technique and don't take part. For me, when a follower of Jesus prays the sinner's prayer again, it's disingenuous, either lying to God or casting doubt on the prior decision to follow Jesus. Maybe his theology requires we renew our salvation commitment every week. Those who prayed the prayer "for the first time" are invited to go to a special place after the service to "get started."

Then someone announces a second collection, this one for the missionary who spoke. The first time we visited, they took two offerings, which I assumed was not typical. Now I wonder if two offerings are their norm. I groan, realizing how right the unchurched are with their complaint that churches are always asking for money. We sing during the offering and stand for the final verse once all the buckets have been picked up.

We sit when the song ends. As a video announcement plays, many people shuffle out. I want to join them but also want to respect the service. The professional cadence and inviting smile of the announcer draws me in. After that, a long series of verbal announcements follow. Mindful of the time and friends we're meeting for lunch, I squirm as the speaker drones on, while more people file out. This is a church where many people arrive late and leave early.

At last, he gives us a blessing and ends the service. With intention, we head for the door, not looking for anyone to interact with, while noting that no one seeks to interact with us. We head for the exit and push into the bitter cold. The biting wind of this winter day cuts through our coats and into our bodies, instantly chilling us.

I so wanted to click with this church, but I so didn't.

Takeaway: For your sake and everyone else's, strive to arrive at church early and leave late—not the opposite.

THE CLOSEST CHURCH

WARM INSIDE

Despite my encouragement, Candy has provided little input on the churches we visit. Though she recommended *The Church with the Fundamental Vibe* and *The Nonconventional Church*, I compiled the rest of the list. Originally containing thirty-five names, I've now cut it in half. While it might be interesting to spend nine months visiting area churches, I lack the patience.

As we move forward, I wonder if we'll add other congregations to our lists of contenders or if visiting more churches will merely delay her selection. I promised that she could pick our next church. I wonder if she already has and is keeping it from me.

Not being part of a specific Christian community gnaws at my soul. Though I maintain my personal spiritual practices of Bible reading and study, prayer, fasting, and writing, my faith flounders. I need, desperately so, to be part of a faith community to provide support and encouragement. I need to receive it, and I long to give it. Without this vital element of spiritual camaraderie, I'm less of a follower of Jesus.

"No man is an island," said John Donne. Now I understand. This realization, however, takes too long for me to recognize, but when I finally do, the need is imperative. While I don't expect church to fill this void, I expect it to stop my downward slide into religious dejection.

Having at last moved into our house, we decide to visit nearby churches. First up is a church a scant six tenths of a mile away. For years I've longed to attend a church in my community where we can gather with our neighbors. Though this church is the closest to us, ideally meeting my first desire, I'm not aware of any neighbors who go there.

Today is unseasonably cold, the coldest day of the winter so far, at -6 °F (-21 °C). The biting wind makes it feel even worse. Though some churches canceled because of the cold, this one did not. In the two minutes it takes to drive there, I forget to pray. Feeling guilty, I mumble a quick petition after I park the car.

The parking lot is vast. With every inch plowed, massive snowbanks line its perimeter. With 90 percent of the lot empty, I chuckle at the futility of clearing the entire space when they need only a small section. Of course, with today's cold weather, some folks will surely stay home. This will make attendance even more sparse.

With the frigid temperature and a much lower wind chill of up to -30 °F (-34 °C), we walk briskly and take shallow breaths so we don't freeze our lungs. The cloudless sky treats us to a bright sunshine, trying to trick us into thinking the day is more pleasant than it is.

Two men greet us just inside the door. Though I don't think they're greeters per se, I do think they're intentional about meeting new people. "Are you new to the area or visiting?"

"We are new to the area, *and* we are visiting," I say.

They welcome us to the neighborhood and to their church. I don't offer my name because I'm waiting to see if they offer theirs. They don't. We make small talk. It's an affable conversation, but they share no information about their church. Pleasant but superficial best describes our encounter. When the conversation wanes, I excuse myself and move further inside the building.

I scan the large narthex. Most everyone appears younger than us, with many thirtysomething couples and their kids. I'm encouraged.

People mill about but no one else seems interested in talking to us. A few folks, however, do smile and give us a welcoming nod. With nothing else to do, we head toward the sanctuary. At the auditorium entrance, a man hands us a bulletin and an information brochure. I thank him with a smile and a downward tip of my head.

With few people sitting, we have our choice of seats. I walk halfway down the center aisle, turn left, and slide midway down the padded pew in the first section.

The area is essentially cube-shaped, with white walls. It

reminds us of some of the United Methodist churches we've visited in the past. Here, offsetting the plain white walls, is too much stained wood trim and some gold-colored embell-ishments, which strike me as pretentious.

Windows abound, letting in much natural light and taking full advantage of today's glorious sunshine. The high cathedral ceiling accentuates the open feel. A few of the windows in the upper front are stained glass, not of the traditional variety, but a more subtle contemporary design. However, a large screen, ready to display elements of the service, blocks our full view of them.

The floor slopes toward the front, with the pews arranged in four sections, allowing room for several hundred people. At about 25 percent full, I wonder how much the weather affected attendance.

Overall, this is a cautiously modern setting, with tradi-tional elements mixed in. I'm not sure how to react to this dichotomy, which is exacerbated by the nontraditional musical instruments on stage.

With a nod to the winter weather, the worship leader welcomes us to start the service. The worship team plays three or four numbers in the opening set. As they move from song to song, the worship leader alternates between guitar and piano. When he moves, the pianist switches over to a keyboard. There's also a drummer and a backup guitarist, who plays various stringed instruments. A trio of back-ground vocalists round out their light pop sound as we sing contemporary songs and choruses.

Next is the children's message. I'm surprised at the

number of kids who flood forward, perhaps twenty-five or thirty. In a church service, the kids are never easy to spot when scanning the crowd, but when they get up for a children's message or to leave for their own activities, their numbers become apparent, often surprising me. Today is such a day.

The minister addresses the kids at their level, while also providing value to the rest of the congregation. He verbally interacts with them, physically involves them, and provides a demonstration for us all. This is not a brief, obligatory activity to check off and move on. It's packed with intention. By the time he dismisses them, we already know the theme of his message and his main point.

The minister has a slight accent, Dutch I assume. At first, I need to focus to catch what he says, but after a few minutes, I no longer notice. This is because of the easy flow of his words, his engaging nature, and the value in what he shares. I immediately like him.

Following the children's message, he promotes a new sermon series for Lent, which he'll start next week, after wrapping up his abbreviated five-week series on the Apostles' Creed today. Next Sunday will feature Holy Communion. He reads a preparatory text to focus our thoughts on that event and the meaning behind it. Then we have a responsive reading of the Ten Commandments, followed by reciting the Apostles' Creed in unison.

From his brief introduction, I assume on week one of the series he summarized the creed, followed by a week for each part of the Trinity: Father, Son, and Holy Spirit. For a denomination that has historically glossed over the work of the Holy Spirit, I'm pleasantly surprised at his inclusion today, being mentioned from the pulpit and in our singing. I wonder if this is normal for them. I hope it is.

Today's message addresses a line in the creed that is often misunderstood and a cause of concern for many: "I believe in the holy catholic Church." This is not a specific nod to the Roman Catholic Church, but instead an acknowledgment to the universal Christian church (which includes Roman Catholicism, along with all of Protestantism).

The key to this delineation is big C Catholic versus small c catholic. The distinction is huge, but it requires explanation for most all who hear this statement of belief from the creed for the first time.

Church, he says, is not a building, a congregation, or a denomination. From the Greek word *Ekklesia*, which is translated *church*, we comprehend it to mean "an assembly of people called out of the world to become part of God's family."

There are two keys to this understanding.

First, we must be united (Matthew 16:18). Second, we must be holy (1 Peter 2:9), The minister defines *holy* as "set apart" and "associated with God". I appreciate this definition of *holy*, as it helps me perceive it as something I can grasp as opposed to something unattainable.

To realize being a universal church, we must be united; we must be one. He hearkens back to his key text for today, Ephesians 4:1–6, which highlights this with the use of *one* seven times.

His message is brilliant and resonates with me, yet, out of necessity, he stops too soon. If we are to truly be a universal church, to be united, to be one, then there is no room for the division caused by our thousands of denominations. Yet he and this church are part of a denomination. The ultimate conclusion in a push for unity is removing denominational distinctions. He doesn't make that statement. In fact, he even attempts to justify denominations. But I don't grasp his explanation. Despite this, he gave a powerful message that I appreciate.

He concludes the service with a short congregational prayer and a lengthy list of announcements. Then he excuses the children for Sunday school. The service ends by taking the offering.

Afterward, coffee and cookies wait for the adults and in fifteen minutes there will be a discussion about the sermon. The opportunity for discussion beckons, but I decide not to. I fear I might blurt out something inappropriate, such as "denominations are the antithesis of church unity." I am their guest, and it's best to keep that thought to myself.

Though the greeting time during the service was one of obligatory routine, afterward people welcome us and talk. They share their names, and we reciprocate. They ask about us and tell us about their church.

I'm pleasantly surprised to spot a neighbor and we talk at length. For years they attended another church, one quite different from this one, but have been coming here for the past few months. He also points out another one of our neighbors I haven't yet met.

As we continue to talk, he makes a vague reference to a

likely future change for this church, assuming that is why we are here today. When I shake my head, he explains. The gist is them joining with another large area church to form something new at this location. The result will be hundreds more people and multiple services, two things that turn me off.

"Why?" I ask.

He shrugs.

Our time together is great, really great. His wife comes up, and we talk as well. Though I want our interaction to continue, their kids grow antsy. I suspect Mom and Dad are ready to leave. I thank them for our conversation and wish them a great rest of the day.

We talk to a few more folks as we head to our car. My expectations for this church were low, but I'm pleased with what I see. For years I've longed to attend church in my neighborhood with my neighbors, to share Christian community *in* my community. This church offers that. Coupled with a great sermon, I add this congregation to my list of contenders.

My wife, however, isn't as enamored. I don't think she's willing to consider them further.

I wonder why she agrees to visit the churches I suggest if she's not interested. Why did we go here today? I fear she's just patiently waiting for me to work through our list of churches, so that once it's completed she can announce the church she's already picked. Am I merely delaying her decision?

Midweek, the pastor emails us, offering to talk or meet if we have questions or would like to learn more. I want to take him up on his offer but don't. Though I'd enjoy getting together, I fear it would raise false expectations on his part.

Takeaway: Seek ways to reach out to visitors: talk with them, form connections, even invite them to meet. And this doesn't just apply to paid staff.

THE TRADITIONAL
DENOMINATIONAL CHURCH
AN EASY NO

As Sunday approaches, I want to return to last week's church. Instead, I refer to our list. The second closest church to our house is another church from a traditional denomination, a short 1.4 miles away. I attended a church in this denomination for the first decade of my life. Later, early in our marriage, Candy and I were members of one for three years.

Based on my experiences, too many churches in this denomination are dying because of aging congregations and few young attendees. *The Outlier Congregation* was a notable exception. Perhaps this church will also be different. To my shock, Candy doesn't balk when I suggest this church. I voice hope. "Maybe we'll be pleasantly surprised."

We don't leave as soon as we should. As a result, we're both frustrated when we get into our car. Only a few seconds into the drive our simmering emotions erupt with raised voices and unkind words. Having mutually expressed our respective angst over some trivial slight, we drive in silence. In another minute we'll be at church, but we haven't yet prayed for the experience. The sad thing is, right now I don't care.

"Do you want to pray for the service?" Candy asks.

No, I don't; I'm mad. I hope she will. After all, she suggested it. "Will you pray?"

"No, I want you to."

I just yelled at my wife. I don't want to talk to anyone, especially not God. Letting out a deep breath, I sigh. "Lord, calm our emotions and prepare us to experience church today. May we receive what you would have us to receive and give what you would have us to give. Open our minds to see what you want to show us. May you be honored by our actions today."

During my short prayer, God soothes my raw emotions and transforms my attitude. I feel better. I'm ready for church. That's good because we're here.

I count six cars in the parking lot. We're number seven. *Great!* I tense a bit, braced for another too-small gathering.

Only after we get out of our car do I see many vehicles parked on the side, too many to count. *That's better.* I relax a little. Though I suspect we should walk around the building to where most of the cars are and seek an entrance there, the biting wind of the winter cold assaults me.

It's not as unseasonably cold as last Sunday, but today the wind pushes the feeling of cold much lower. I want to get inside as fast as I can. I follow a few footprints in the snow to the closest door. It's at a lower level than the main entrance in the front, and I wonder where it might lead.

It's not a welcoming approach. I brace myself to tug on a locked door. To my relief the door yields to my gentle pull, depositing us on a landing midpoint on a stairway. We walk up several steps and find ourselves in the narthex, a pleasant and warm space. A lady heading to the stairs welcomes us with a smile. But she has no time to talk, she explains, because she's headed to work in the nursery. I'm encouraged. Despite seeing only senior citizens milling about, the need for a nursery suggests younger families attend too.

We saunter in. Already I know I won't like this church or our experience here. This isn't a snap determination made with premature rashness but a reasoned judgment resulting from the scores of churches we've visited over the past few years. Based on what I've seen so far, I can predict with high accuracy what the people and service will be like. *Why are we here? Why did we bother?* I want to leave.

Meandering toward the sanctuary, we look for someone to talk to or someone looking to talk to us. No one notices. We're invisible—again. I look for coatracks but don't see any. Although slightly irked, I'm okay keeping my coat on. Despite only a brief exposure to the winter chill, it will take time for my body to warm.

While I'm looking for a coatrack, Candy seeks a bulletin. This is definitely a bulletin-type church, but she can't find one. Now she's irked too. The pews have padded seats but aren't nearly as nice as last week's. I squirm, trying to get comfortable.

The character of the building reminds me of 1960-style construction, but it's nicely maintained and doesn't feel that old. Though there are few windows, the space is well lit, giving an open, inviting ambiance. The stage, however, has the strangest array of decorations, giving off an almost spooky vibe. It's surreal, and I try to ignore it. I know someone put a lot of effort into this, but the results are bizarre.

Candy still looks for bulletins, finally spotting a rack of them by one of the side aisles. After she leaves to retrieve one, an older lady approaches me from the other side. With a smile, she hands me a bulletin. "Here, you might want one of these."

I thank her, and she nods. That's the end of our exchange, but I'm pleased she made the effort.

Candy returns, with bulletin in hand, and a man—the first person we've seen younger than ourselves—walks up to us. He introduces himself and we have an extended conversation. Our exchange, however, is uncomfortable because he's standing and we're sitting. *Why didn't I stand too?* Nevertheless, his outreach honors me.

We've now had three interactions with people at this church. Each one felt awkward, yet I prefer uneasy conversation to no conversation. No one wants to be ignored. (I must admit I could have contributed to the discomfort of each situation.)

I estimate the church seats about 350 and is less than half full. Though all age groups are present, the crowd skews toward the senior citizen demographic. The front five rows are completely empty in each of the four sections, with most people packed into the back of the sanctuary. Though we're only a fourth of the way in, as many people sit behind us as in front.

We keep our coats on. I squirm trying to find a comfortable position in the uncomfortable pew.

"Look, there's a drum set." Candy points with a subtle tip of her head. "It's hidden behind the piano." Drums seem so out of place in this traditional setting. I wonder if they will be part of today's service. I don't need to wonder long.

With a pleasant smile, a man approaches the piano. An accomplished pianist, he plays the prelude and then invites the worship team forward. Four vocalists pick up mics as they fan out along the front of the stage. A woman sits at a keyboard behind the piano, and a twenty-something guy goes to the sequestered drum kit, housed in a Plexiglas enclosure.

They open with a contemporary song, followed by an obligatory greeting time. Though we shake hands or wave at everyone around us, the most anyone says is "Hi" or "Welcome." The intention is good, but the results are superficial. I feel like a poser, a fraud. I smile and pretend to be happy, just like everyone else, but we're acting as if we're all friends, when in reality we're strangers—except for the one man we talked to when we first sat.

We sing two more songs, one contemporary and the other a hymn. The congregational prayer follows. As a kid I learned to ignore these lengthy recitations of congregational needs, and I never broke that habit. The prayer drones on.

Afterward he dismisses the kids. It's too late. They should have been released before the boring prayer, lest they, too, learn to ignore it as I did. Then the ushers take two offerings in rapid succession. Though many people sit in front of us, the first bucket goes by with only a few bills in the bottom. The second one is empty. Either this is a stingy church, or they give their offerings in other ways. Singing during the collections, we stand for the final verse once the ushers have completed their task. At last, I'm warm enough to take off my coat.

The sermon is part of a series from the book of James. The pastor is a contract minister; they just extended his agreement six months while they seek a permanent replacement. He reads James 5:7–20. He's a polished presenter who communicates with ease. The title of his message is "The Quest for Christian Maturity: In Patience and Prayer."

We are impatient, he says. Consider Moses, Abraham and Sarah, and Peter. "Patience produces fruit, gives testimony, and reveals God's care." With three points for part one, I wonder if this was once a sermon by itself. "Without trials," he concludes, "there would be no perseverance; without battle, no victory."

For the second half on prayer, there are likewise three points. We pray "in difficult circumstances, in sickness, and in spiritual struggle."

What about prayers of confession, thanksgiving, and praise? We need those types of prayers too. Surely God must tire of us only asking for things.

"Prayer is getting God's will done on earth," he says in

conclusion. This sounds nice, but I wonder if it has biblical support.

He says a closing prayer and dismisses us.

We move slowly and are the last to leave the sanctuary. Some people give us a passing nod, others thank us for visiting, and a few invite us back. But no one shares their names or asks ours. No one attempts conversation. I wonder if they expect their paid clergy to do that.

The minister stands dutifully at the sanctuary's main exit. With no one behind us, we tarry. I tell him we are new to the area and visiting local churches, but I think he assumes we've already selected this one. He tells us about their evening service and where the church is in their process of finding a new minister. He's a nice man, and I like him, but we don't plan to come back, so I doubt we'll ever see him again.

Candy asks if I want to hang out in the narthex to see if there's anyone we can talk to. I see no point in trying and am okay to leave. I think she's relieved. As we head toward the door, though, we have one final interaction. It's the best of the whole morning. Two ladies take time to learn about us and share about themselves. One woman is the mother of the man we talked to before the service, and the other is the fill-in pastor's wife. Both are nice ladies, and I appreciate them reaching out to us. As we say our goodbyes, they both invite us back.

Candy and I don't talk about the experience on our short drive home. Later I ask what she thought, but she has little to share. I already know and didn't need to ask: She didn't like it and doesn't want to return. I agree.

Last week's sermon elevated the Holy Spirit to an equal level with the other parts of the Trinity; this week's message ignored him. Last week I enjoyed our church experience; this week, I didn't. I wonder if there's a connection.

Takeaway: Look for ways to welcome visitors and give them a reason to come back.

THE FUNDAMENTAL CHURCH
LIFE GROUPS VS SUNDAY SCHOOL

E arly this morning we make our annual switch to Daylight Saving Time, a transition full of folly and one I wish we'd skip. I wake up tired. I don't want to roll out of bed and so want to skip church, but I know Candy won't stand for it.

"What church are we going to," she asks, "and when does it start?"

"Next on the list is the church just north of us . . . 9:30."

"When should we leave, 9:15?"

The drive will only take two minutes, and I don't care if we arrive early or not. Even leaving at 9:25 will be fine, but it's good to pad our schedule because one of us is bound to be late, so I nod my agreement.

"We better get moving."

I wonder aloud if today we should pick a different church, one that starts later. Even 10:00 will help, but Candy shakes off my suggestion.

Considering my morning routine, I should pare back my activities so I don't have to rush to make church. But that would mean cutting out my morning prayer time and Bible study. It seems foolish to skip personal intimacy with God just to make it to church on time.

Another idea is omitting my shower, but I need its warm comfort to feel awake and act civilized. Bypassing breakfast is another thought, but I know I should limit fasting to when I'm not around other people because sometimes an empty stomach makes me less patient. Of all my considerations, church is the least significant. I could skip it. I've now come full circle in my deliberations.

In the end, I try to squeeze in everything.

Diligent, I push forward: prayer, Bible reading, breakfast, and a shower. I emerge from the bathroom breathless, ready for church and thinking I'm on schedule. I'm not. My wife stands by the back door with her coat on.

It's 9:25. *We can do this.*

Two days ago, I began my weekend construction project by hitting my thumb with a hammer. Hard. Since then, it's hampered everything I've done. Even the slightest touch to my tender digit shoots pain through my body. Unfortunately, many common motions qualify. These include holding my car keys, reaching into my pocket, turning on my cell phone, buttoning buttons, and tying shoes.

Anxious to get out the door, I pull on my boots with haste, jamming my thumb into the stiff leather. I yelp. On a scale of one to ten, the pain is at eleven. I curse. Always inappropriate, my words seem even more unholy given that in a few minutes I'll be at church to worship God. Tears well up in my eyes as my thumb throbs, perhaps even worse now than when I first injured it. Gingerly, I lace my boots and tie them with care. Reaching into my pocket for my keys, I jam my thumb again. The tenderness is excruciating. I set my jaw to prevent another errant outburst, but my glare says it anyway.

The drive to church is tense. Knowing that I'm in no mood to pray, my wise bride intercedes for our time at church.

We pull into the lot from a side entrance and park in the back of an elongated facility sporting multiple additions. The clock in the car tells me it's 8:28. Mentally adjusting for Daylight Saving Time, we have two minutes before church starts.

Ahead of us, one couple scurries in a back door, but we don't follow them. Another family heads toward the front of the building. We trail behind, entering through a side door that deposits us into the narthex. The service has begun. I scan for a coatrack but don't see one. I head to the sanctuary with Candy following.

With people everywhere, we stand in a daze. There are no seats available in the back for us to slide into. A smiling usher hands Candy a bulletin and offers to help us find a place for two. Seeing plenty of spaces further in, I push forward. Halfway up, I slide into the center section and move in a few spaces.

Sitting, I take a deep breath, which serves as a wordless prayer that Papa hears and graciously answers. I forget our late arrival, my throbbing thumb, and the unholy drama that surrounded it. I am ready for church.

The building is large, with comfortable padded chairs for over four hundred. It's half full, mostly seniors, with some young adults but hardly any kids. Many of the older men wear suits, with some ladies in dresses, but the rest of the crowd dresses more casually.

After the opening remarks, which occurred as we walked in, there's the official greeting time. I shake hands and exchange hellos with the young man next to me, surprising him when I ask, "How are you?"

Stunned, he does a double take and gives a socially acceptable response but then quickly turns away as if uncomfortable with my unexpected question. As an experiment, I try this with everyone I greet. None of them are ready for anything beyond "Hello."

Next, we sing an opening three-song set. In addition to a suit-clad worship leader are three vocalists and a bass guitar, all on stage. On the sides are the organist, pianist, keyboardist, and drummer. They start the first song before the bass guitarist is ready, but it doesn't matter because I can't hear him when he does start to play. The piano and organ carry the music, with an out-of-place percussionist tapping a rhythm that doesn't seem to fit with what everyone else does.

The group's light pop sound from a bygone era feels out of place with their hymns and older choruses. Without hymnals, we follow along with the words displayed overhead. Only about half the crowd sings, and they do it with little enthusiasm.

For the second song, the worship leader straps on a guitar. A man wearing a suit while playing a guitar looks strange. Though he acts comfortable with this dichotomy, it strikes me as odd. The third song, "Amazing Grace," garners full participation from the crowd, the only number to do so.

An offertory prayer precedes the collection, which coincides with a special music number. The soloist sings as ushers pass the plates. But few people add anything to the offering. When the man finishes his song, applause erupts. Since this is the only clapping all morning, I assume the praise is for him and not for God.

Next week starts their two-week missions festival. Today serves as the warm-up, with a message titled, "What Is a Call?" Though his delivery is good, the preacher is hard for me to watch. When he's not looking down, he fixes his gaze over us, as though he's watching something behind us and ignoring us. I desperately want to turn around to see what he sees, but I resist the urge.

For the bulk of his message, he reels through a list of biblical characters and what God called them to do. He emphasizes, "God calls people in turn," but I'm not sure what he means. It's not until he nears the end of his message that he mentions the text for today, Ephesians 2:8–10.

He wraps up with three practical, self-help style tips to discern our calling. Though disappointed he didn't mention hearing our call from the Holy Spirit, I'm not surprised. We're at a quintessential fundamentalist church and not a charismatic gathering. I'm quite used to churches ignoring one third of the Trinity.

He closes the service with prayer and invites us to stay for "life groups." I'm surprised at his mention of the more modern life group phenomenon. I'm perplexed at them taking place when most traditional churches hold Sunday school.

As we slowly gather our things to leave, a suit-wearing man of our age introduces himself. He, too, invites us to stay for life groups. "In fact, I teach one of them." He beams, expecting we'll jump at the chance. His smile disappears when I decline.

His assertion that life groups have an instructor confuses me. Life groups, as I know them, don't have a teacher. Though some groups might have a leader or facilitator, many are egalitarian and there's seldom a lesson. I wonder if their label of "life groups" is a ruse, merely attempting to put a new spin on the old practice of Sunday school.

I don't need to wonder long. An older woman walks by us as she defiantly declares, "I'm going to Sunday school!" I smile at her honesty.

All the people sitting around us have scattered. None of those I greeted—those I dared to ask, "How are you?"—tarry to say "Goodbye" or invite us back.

One elderly man approaches us as we're about to leave. We actually talk, sharing information and learning about each other. This one person attempts to connect with us. He warms my heart. As we say our goodbyes, he invites us back and hopes we'll return. His sincerity touches me.

In the short drive home, we discuss our experience. I'm

critical over some sloppy details in the preacher's message. Candy is more generous. We both agree, however, that we connected with his main premise about knowing our call.

I'm not interested in returning to this church and don't want to give them further consideration. However, I'm unsure of Candy's perspective. This church is like the one we met at and the churches she attended growing up. I'm relieved when she shakes her head.

We pull into the garage. There's only one thing left to do: reset the clock in the car to Daylight Saving Time. Lunch and a nap await us inside.

Takeaway: Don't put a new label on something old and think you've made a meaningful change. Instead, make changes that matter.

THE CHURCH WITH A FRESH SPIN
BREATHING LIFE INTO OLD PRACTICES

The three churches nearest to us—*The Closest Church*, *The Traditional Denominational Church*, and *The Fundamental Church*—all have traditional-sounding names, meet in traditional-looking buildings, and have traditional-style services. This church, only 1.8 miles away and just past *The Fundamental Church*, boasts a nontraditional name. Though their building still looks like a church, it's not as typical. I wonder if their service will likewise break from status quo religion.

They are from the same denomination as *The Outlier Congregation* and *The Traditional Denominational Church*. I wonder which one they'll be more like. At last, we can find out.

On a corner, I'm not sure where their drive is. Candy points straight ahead, but I turn the corner. Only then do we see a drive off each street. A small church bus drops off riders under the awning that shelters the main entrance. I wheel around and park in a nearby space, eager to get inside. Candy is in less of a hurry.

Greeted at the door, the man knows we're visitors and welcomes us warmly. Inside, many more acknowledge our presence with a nod, a wave, or a handshake. No one asks if we're visiting. They all know. What several ask is if we're new to the area, while a few cautiously inquire if we're looking for a church.

We move into the sanctuary, which the shape of a gymnasium. A high open ceiling, painted black, and dark walls provide a spartan feel, while the well-lit, laid-back atmosphere draws me in. Round tables, circled with chairs, fill the back and partway up the sides, while rows of folding chairs line the front.

The pastor, in casual attire and with an unassuming persona, welcomes us. He shares his first name but doesn't reveal his title. I'm so pleased to meet a minister who doesn't need to tie his identity with what he does or his credentials. This man possesses both the confidence and the humility to be Gene, a person just like me, without any label to erect an unbiblical distinction between us. I immediately like him.

The tables are inviting, but I don't want to sit on the periphery. I yearn to be closer to the action. We move toward the middle of the room, sliding into a center row. As Candy reads the bulletin, I check out the space. It's accessible and comfortable, feeling as much like a pleasant place to hang out as it does a church. Unlike last week, with its predominance of seniors, there are few here today. What I see is a nice range of ages and many kids. Judging by their smiles and laughter, the congregation is excited to be here, eager for the service to begin. Anticipation permeates the room.

The worship team gathers on stage, elevated by three short steps. Forming a tight circle, they bow their heads in a posture of intercession. Their example reminds me of what I neglected to do. In anticipation of my visit, I forgot to pray on our way here. Candy didn't suggest it either. I now bow my head.

The seven people on stage scatter to their positions. A tall man straps on a guitar and opens the service. Around him are a trumpet player, a keyboardist on an electric organ, a drummer, and three female vocalists. Their sound is upbeat and inviting, something quite different from last week. They lead us in singing contemporary choruses and one updated hymn.

After the opening song set is the official greeting time. This is not the typical moment of rote interaction but an extended period that allows real connections to occur. Then we sing some more.

The pastor publicly appears for the first time, asking for people to come forward to pray for him and the service. Two people do. I'm pleased to see the laity pray for the congregation and their minister as part of the service. What a fine example they set.

Behind the stage hangs some remarkable artwork, which guides their Lenten services. Reminiscent of the "Stations of the Cross," an eight-panel mosaic shows Jesus's journey toward his sacrificial death and ultimate resurrection. Today is panel four, "Gethsemane." Referring to Mark 14:32–42, a three-part sermon emerges about reaffirmation, restoration, and revelation.

The pastor, we learn, meets each Thursday morning with a group of guys. There he previews the text for Sunday's service. He goes there as a participant, not a leader or teacher. His goal is to listen to their discussion. Some of the men's insights end up in his message. This is just one of the many small tweaks this church makes from the norm of status quo Sunday services. Collectively, these changes add up to provide a fresh experience for me.

He ends his message with a prayer and what I think is the closing song. Then they take an offering, during which is an "open mic" time. I cringe a bit, as I've often seen these go terribly wrong. Invariably someone, either well-intentioned or with an agenda, hijacks the mic and subjects the congregation to a barely coherent story or a passionate rant about something few others care about. Still, I like their bravery to try it, knowing that when this works, it works extremely well.

A young man comes forward, sharing what turns out to be a lengthy set of announcements about the youth group, which seems connected with Young Life. I like them tapping an available resource and not trying to reproduce what already exists.

Another man follows him to talk about a recent short-term mission trip he was on, but I think his real goal is to recruit more people for future trips. Then the pastor prays for things mentioned by both people.

But the service isn't over.

The minister asks for "prayer servants" to come forward. This may have been the same term he used when soliciting prayer before his message. Two people stand.

Two others rove the audience with handheld mics as people share their needs and joys. After each person speaks, one of the prayer servants intercedes. As the people reveal what's on their hearts, I pray silently for them too. Eight people seek prayer. This is a caring, praying congregation that puts biblical faith into action. I so like that.

Now the service is officially over, but the interaction isn't. Although people prepare to leave, few hurry off. Many tarry to talk, some interacting with us. Most of these conversations are short, but a couple are more intentional, and one is in depth.

Though part of a traditional denomination, this congregation has made several intentional adjustments in their practices to put a fresh spin on old customs, departing from the status quo in enough areas to entice me. Although I desire an experience that breaks completely with the routines of today's church culture to reclaim the mindset of the early church, I realize I may not find such a group.

I want to come back.

My wife sees only this church's connections with their stodgy denomination and can't move past it. It could be her insight is more accurate than mine. Unlike me, she has no interest in returning. Once was enough.

She makes her pronouncement with enough finality that I know we won't return.

Takeaway: Look for ways to put a fresh spin on old customs to be more relevant for today's visitors.

THE MYSTERY CHURCH
A MARKETING FAILURE

The last four churches have been the closest to our house and all are part of our local community. There is one more church that's nearby. It's two miles away. In the brief time we've been in the area, the name of the church has changed. Its original occupants first migrated to a coffee house that's closed on Sundays. Then they left that venue and disappeared.

Replacing them in their old building is another church from an adjoining community. They sold their facility and are renting this one—so say online news reports. Because they've recently moved from another area, I expect the congregation likewise hails from other places and don't expect that any neighbors attend there.

No one we've talked to knows anything about this church.

All we know is their name and location. There are no service times posted on their sign, and they have no website.

A basic Facebook page has a couple of pictures and posts, but nothing gives service times or contact information. The most recent post invites people to their Christmas Eve service, which occurred several months ago.

It could be they've closed. Or they're closed to visitors since they're secretive of their service times and contact information. Who knows?

So aside from a desire to experience all the churches in our community, I don't want to visit this one—even if I could. I share my feelings with Candy. She agrees to skip it.

Takeaway: Make it easy for people to learn about your church. This includes service times and who to contact with questions.

THE MULTISITE CHURCH
AN INNOVATIVE APPROACH

Removing *The Mystery Church* from our schedule leaves us with a last-minute quandary of where to go this Sunday. Candy recalls that one of our neighbors and her husband attend church in the community east of us. My bride contacts her online, and we soon have the details we need.

The initial information about this church surprises me. They have three Sunday morning services: 8:00, 9:30, and 11:15. Though some of the area's larger churches have two morning services, this is the first we've heard of with three. *How big is this church, anyway?*

We pick the middle service, and our neighbors confirm that's the one they attend. I wonder if we'll be able to find them in what is likely to be a large crowd.

Intrigued, I go online. I find an easy-to-use website, with all the needed information, including a helpful FAQ section under the "I'm New" tab. They're part of a multisite network of churches started by one of the area's larger denominational churches, whose main site alone borders on being a megachurch. We visited it several years ago with our son and daughter-in-law when they first moved to the area. Though the service was neither traditional nor formal, it carried the vibe of both, feeling constrained within a contemporary setting.

The founding church began their pursuit of multisite a few years ago, now having five congregations. How churches handle multisite varies, from essentially independent to watching a video feed from the main location and everything in between. Some multisite churches have the music and other aspects of the service local, with the message piped in. I wonder which flavor we'll experience, hoping we won't be watching the entire thing on a giant screen.

As we leave our subdivision, we meet another set of neighbors headed north, while we head south. "I wonder where they're going to church?" As we continue driving, we cross paths with many people, dressed for church but all headed in different directions.

"Look at that," I tell Candy. "Everyone heads someplace different for church. Why can't we all attend church in our own community?" The whole thing is absurd, but she feels the same way about my comment.

Soon we're at church. I turn into the drive where we're greeted by a flag-wielding parking lot attendant who motions me right. To see if he's paying attention, I smile and wave as I drive by. He reciprocates. Another man signals us onward to where a third directs us to our parking spot.

Although they guide us to a parking space with exacting precision, we don't know which door to enter. A quick glance reveals three options, with people streaming toward two of them.

The closest door is more logical, both in terms of proximity and building position, yet the one further away is grander. That's where we head.

Inside is the din of people as they mill about. There are no greeters to welcome us. No one says "Hi" or acknowledges our presence. We blend into the mass of people, so I don't expect anyone to approach us as visitors—or to even know we're visiting.

We float anonymous in a surging sea of humanity, albeit one exuding excitement over spending time together and worshiping God. Today is Palm Sunday. I wonder if the day carries heightened excitement or if this is normal.

Though the lobby space is not small, the throng of people navigating it make it crowded. A couple small tables offer an assortment of baked goods. I'm not sure if these are for the first-service crowd, who has by now mostly departed, or for new arrivals. Candy checks out the goodies but takes nothing, while I scan for a coatrack. Not seeing one, or even the hint of where to look, I resign to keep my winter coat with me even though few others have. We snake our way through the crowd toward the sanctuary that looms in front of us.

The facility has a typical large-church auditorium: pleasant, yet utilitarian, smartly finished with no hint of ostentatious fluff. It reminds me of last week's meeting space, only on a newer, larger scale. It seats about 650. I find it quite comfortable.

I walk halfway up the aisle and slide in four seats. Candy sits next to me with a questioning look. "I left two seats for our neighbors," I explain, "just in case we see them." Out of hundreds of people, we know we won't.

She smiles at my hopefulness but then moments later spots them a couple rows forward across the aisle. The wife beckons us to join them, and we do. We exchange introductions and chat as we wait for the service to start.

Sitting with people we know, even though just a bit, is comforting—and comfortable. This only heightens my expectations for the morning. However, I'm also mindful that at nine miles away, there are scores of churches closer to us.

After criticizing others for driving past some churches to attend another one, part of me will feel guilty if I like this church better than the options in our community. I don't have long to contemplate this, however, as the service begins. The sanctuary is mostly full, and the clang of folding chairs being set up in the back suggests more people arriving and in need of a seat.

Tim, the lead pastor for this site, welcomes us to this service. He gives a brief teaching about Palm Sunday, weaving seeker-sensitive language into more typical church jargon. I wonder, however, if an uninitiated visitor would find his explanation accessible or confusing. To me it's a bit jarring as he switches between fresh wording for familiar concepts and common Christianese verbiage. He also specifically addresses visitors, giving a brief overview of the church before the worship team takes over for the next part of the service.

Seven people, with guitars, drums, and keyboard, lead us in worship, singing a modern song and then a hymn for their first set. I don't know either song and find them hard to sing. My wife feels they drag on for too long, with too much repetition. The worship leader is skilled and the instrumentation mixes nicely for a contemporary sound with the hint of an edge, but the vocals don't flow, calling attention to certain individuals when they should be blending.

Tim pops up again, this time for announcements, including reeling off a packed schedule for Holy Week, culminating in the Easter celebration next Sunday. I can't keep track of all the options and soon stop listening.

Somewhere in the mix, we greet one another. Though everyone is polite and tries to welcome all those around them, just as instructed, they do so with a honed brevity: a smile, a handshake, and a "Hello" before peeling off to repeat the ritual with the next person.

I throw off the cadence of several folks when I interject a "How are you?" into their routine. Though they politely reciprocate, no one takes this as a hint for more conversation. No one shares their name or asks mine. They're friendly without reaching out. Even though I'm disappointed, I realize that, despite their shortcomings, they greet better than most of the churches we visit. With barely enough time to spin around to address the seven people within reach, the time for friendliness ends.

Tim introduces the offering, telling visitors not to "feel obligated," while imploring regulars, almost to the point of begging, to "give generously." I wonder how visitors feel about his instructions. The ushers pass deep baskets to receive the donations, while the worship team leads us in another song. It's unfamiliar to me, but most people here seem to know it well.

Afterward, another man stands to give the message. We learn he isn't their regular speaker, just an occasional one. I wonder if he might rotate among the different congregations in their network. He's a gifted communicator, easy to listen to, and engaging. He'll wrap up the sermon series, "The Good Life," based on Psalm 23. Today he focuses on the second half of verse 5, with the title, "He Anoints My Head."

"Have you ever done something you don't normally do," he asks, "just so you can be accepted?" God exists in community, and he made us to want the same thing. "Belonging is good."

He weaves stories from the Bible into his teaching as he moves the idea of acceptance forward. He ends his message with the reminder that we don't need to do anything for God to accept us. It's all about his grace, not our efforts.

He concludes with some thought-provoking questions and closes with prayer. The worship team leads us in a final song, a contemporary number that we know well. The service ends.

I stand and put on my coat, slowly turning to look at those I greeted earlier in the service. I seek someone to interact with, but no one notices. Candy talks with our neighbor.

As I try to listen in on their conversation, a woman

approaches me with intention. I don't recognize her but think I should. She introduces herself and tells me where they live. It all clicks. I met her and her family last fall. I smile. "We passed each other on the way to church. You headed north as we headed south." She looks confused, but her husband nods. We had waved to each other.

We have a joyful time connecting. They make me feel like I belong, as part of the community. Besides them and the neighbors we sat with, they say our next-door neighbors also go here, but to the third service.

I marvel at what I've just learned. Although in a different community, three of our neighbors attend this church. This is more than any of the other churches we've visited. As I contemplate this, they say that their parent church wants to open another location and is in discussion for a partnership with *The Closest Church*, the option nearest to our home.

This explains the vague information I received when we visited there, about the possibility of them joining forces with another church that would bring hundreds more people to their location and result in multiple services. I now understand what might happen and see how it could function.

If this transpires, I wonder if our neighbors who go to this church would switch to the one closer to our homes. Despite me desiring a smaller church community and not wanting to be part of a large gathering, if several of our neighbors went here, it would make a significant difference.

This church has much to offer. I'm interested in return-ing, though I suspect Candy isn't. When I ask about her thoughts, she complains over a comment the minister made about a social issue. I missed it. My wife didn't. Though she wants to go to a church not afraid to address social issues, what they say about the issues is just as important. This pastor's view doesn't align with hers. This one comment is her chief memory of the service.

Takeaway: Consider how your church addresses social issues. Should you ignore them or stand up for what you believe?

THE CHURCH WITH GOOD MUSIC
WAITING FOR THE SERVICE TO START

I volunteer at a budget program where I teach classes and encourage people to manage their finances, unlearn bad money-handling habits, and dig out of debt. It's a biblically based program, and it meets at a local church, which is also today's destination.

In the brief time I've been involved, the budgeting program has grown significantly. I have mixed feelings about this. Part of me is glad we're meeting the needs of more people in the community, but I'm also dismayed at the demand. I wish I could work myself out of a job, but according to Jesus that will never happen. He said there will always be poor people who need help (Mark 14:7).

I'm pleased this church provides space for the program. I'm sure this comes from a desire to make a difference in their community, something all churches should do but that too few pursue with any degree of effort or success.

It's also an example of good stewardship. Nearly all

church buildings sit idle most of the week, so anything that increases occupancy expands the reach of the church and honors the donations of the people who made the facility possible. I'm sure this pleases God too.

The pastor of this church teaches a Bible class as part of the budgeting program, so I've met him a few times, and we've had some brief conversations. However, I've not told him I plan to visit this church. I think our daughter and son-in-law might like it, so I invite them to meet us.

Though I'm open to this being our future church home, I'm doubtful. It's not as close to our house as I'd like, and I don't think any neighbors go here. I wonder if it will appeal to Candy. Regardless, I expect to better understand the church and their services. This will allow me to tell clients at the budgeting classes about it if they have questions. Though most clients already have a church connection, some don't. I want to help those folks find a church home, and this one would be an obvious choice since they already come here during the week for budgeting classes.

I know it takes exactly fifteen minutes to drive there, and we depart ten minutes before that, allowing time for possible pre-church interaction. We leave on schedule, and I pray for our time at this church. My wife is grumbling a bit, however. She didn't have time to brew a cup of coffee before we left, so she gave up her morning routine to keep us on schedule. Her decision pleases me.

On other occasions she's persisted in making her hot beverage when we should have been leaving. In those instances, I've not been patient, with us invariably arriving at church late and with me frustrated. This won't happen today.

With our pre-church prayer going before us, the drive is pleasant. It's a nice spring day, with warm sunshine, increasing temperatures, and a gentle breeze. We pull into the lot ten minutes early. There aren't many cars. My expectations sink. Though more park in the side lot, this isn't the bustling church I expected.

The rest of our family isn't here yet, so we move with deliberate slowness. We head inside, standing in the narthex as we scope things out. To our left is the sanctuary. Though an usher stands at the door, the room is empty except for the sound guys in back and the worship team up front. To our right are classrooms, along with most of the activity.

Candy spies some coffee and heads toward it. As she prepares her concoction, I stand alone. People scurry past. I try to make eye contact, but no one notices. No one stops to chat or even wave a hello. Once again, I'm alone in a room full of people. I expected better.

With coffee now in my bride's hand, we have nothing else to do, so we head toward the sanctuary. With every chair empty, the usher encourages us to wait. "Most people don't come in until after the service starts," he says with a smile. This bothers me—a lot. This practice suggests other things are more important to these folks than preparing to worship God. Even though he should be their focus, they place other activities first, and he comes second.

If people would talk to me, I'd gladly wait. Maybe the usher will, since he has nothing else to do at the moment. I extend my hand to shake his and introduce myself. He reciprocates and hands me a bulletin. So much for conversation.

After we sit, the minister spots us and comes over to greet us. I'm so excited for some interaction that I forget to introduce Candy. "There will only be about fifteen people here when the service starts," he says with a smile, "but by the end of the second song, there will be about forty." I nod. "There are about one hundred at our second service."

Looking around, I suspect the place seats about 150. "It would be crowded if you just had one service." This time he's the one to nod.

"We encourage people to serve during one service and attend the other." I wonder how many do. He again thanks us for visiting and excuses himself.

I spot our family in the narthex and go to meet them. Someone is explaining the nursery options, but they decide to keep their son with them. I hold out my hands, and he comes to me. As I carry him into the sanctuary, the music plays. His body responds to the beat. "Do you like the music?"

"Yeah."

"There are guitars," Candy says. "Do you like guitars?"

"Yeah!" He nods and then starts bobbing his little head.

By the time his mother joins us, he's ready to go back to her. After a few minutes he reaches for his dad. Then back to her. It's a game for him, but they don't want to play. They take him to the nursery.

The music is upbeat, possibly the most engaging of all the churches so far. The worship leader plays guitar, with two more on guitars and one on bass. A drummer and keyboardist round out the ensemble, with a young woman singing backup. Some instrumentalists are also miked for vocals. Their voices blend nicely, with the sound superbly balanced. Though the newness of the situation distracts me, I'm drawn into worshiping God. Musical excellence is one of Candy's requirements for our next church. I wonder if this qualifies.

After two contemporary songs come announcements and a time to greet those around us. As predicted, our numbers have now swelled to about forty or more. Though we sit in the second row from the back in the front section, no one sits in front of us. Most people pick the middle section. With the only people to greet sitting behind us, I turn to the young couple behind me. Though they aren't prepared for it, I try to draw them into conversation. We just start to connect when the music resumes and halts our inter-action. We sing an old hymn, updated to work with their modern instruments, followed by another contemporary song. I enjoy the singing.

Communion is next. The bulletin notes, "All believers may take part," addressing my most pressing question. Then, perhaps for our benefit, the minister thoroughly explains their process. He succinctly addresses every other question anyone could have about how they practice the Lord's Supper. Never have I had Communion at a church I visited when I fully knew what to expect, how I fit in, what to do, and when I should do it. Without uncertainty getting in my way, I'm able to contemplate Jesus's amazing gift to us as I partake in this ritual he started two thousand years ago.

The offering follows. The pastor excuses visitors from

participating and then implores members to give and to give generously. His entreaty borders on pleading. First, they take a collection for their general fund, and then they take a second one, but I don't catch the designated cause. I'm irked at how often churches in this area take two collections during their services. As I've already mentioned, this further reinforces the claims of the unchurched that "churches are always asking for money."

The sermon is part of a series, "Breaking Free," from the book of Exodus. Today's topic is "Getting to Know God," with Exodus 3:13–15 as our text. The pastor is easy to listen to, but his style confounds me. He doesn't provide us with three points or give a message that allows for easy note taking. Instead, his talk takes us on a meandering journey with interconnected thoughts that loop and intersect and repeat. I enjoy listening to him but cannot corral his words into a succinct summary. Even with the fill-in-the-blank sheet in the bulletin, I'm not able to subject his words to an order that satisfies my logical-thinking mind.

"We are each known by different names . . . and by different attributes," I write. So is God. When Moses asks God, "Who should I say sent me?" God merely says, "I AM." The minister voices what has always exasperated me. "This explains nothing; it doesn't help at all."

Yahweh, he adds, is represented as LORD in the Bible. I never knew that—or I forgot. I'm glad for the insight.

"We are not the center, the focus, or in control," he says. "God is." He wants us to know him. Moses knew God and radiated his glory. "Our job," the minister later adds, "is to reflect God's glory." This one line is my key takeaway, his

main point for the message. By the time he ends, I feel sati-
ated but can't explain why.

He concludes with the subtlest of invitations, a ritual I
learned to ignore after five years at an evangelical church.
After a closing prayer, the worship team treats us to a
resonating reprise of their opening number. The powerful
music draws me to God as the words resound in my mind.

After the worship leader dismisses us, we talk some more
with the couple who sat behind us and another couple who
joined them after the greeting time. As we file out, the
minister stands by the exit, smiling and shaking hands.

This isn't a rote exercise. He's bonding with people,
caring for his flock. I want to communicate my sincere
appreciation for the way he explained their Communion
practice, but my words refuse to form when the time comes.
I could honestly tell him I enjoyed his message but am not
sure how to do so without it sounding like an obligatory
compliment. Instead, I just smile, and he thanks me for
being here today.

I nod. "It was good to be here." And it was.

In the narthex, one of their worship team members
introduces himself. He works with our son-in-law. We talk at
length, connecting, meeting his family, and learning about
his journey. Our conversation is even better than the church
service.

This is why I go to church: to connect with other
followers of Jesus, to enjoy meaningful spiritual conversations, and to experience true fellowship—without coffee and
cookies to detract from forming real relationships. The
extended conversation lasts until music signals the start of

the second service. Our new acquaintance scurries off to join the rest of the worship team.

We walk outside. The sun is shining, but the wind now has a bite. I long to bask in the warm rays while simultaneously desiring to escape the bitter gusts.

We decide to have an early lunch and head to a quick-serve restaurant. As we enjoy our burgers and fries, my mind is still on church. "I think that was the best music of the churches we've visited." Candy agrees, both surprising and pleasing me, but that's all she has to say. Our daughter and son-in-law remain noncommittal about the experience, neither gushing with praise nor criticizing the service. Maybe they need time to process it.

The next day our daughter shares more: the music was good, but not as good as our former church. I'm resigned to not being able to find music that matches that church; perhaps our former church doesn't even align with our memories of our time there. Besides, picking a church based on music, while understandable, is shortsighted. When the music wanes, will you leave?

"If you decide to go there," she concludes, "we may go with you once in a while."

Takeaway: Church practices that seem normal and self-explanatory to regular attendees—such as Communion—may confuse or confront visitors. Be sure to let them know what will happen and how they can take part.

THE SIMULCAST CHURCH

TWO OPTIONS IN ONE BUILDING

T he budget program I'm involved with on Wednesday mornings also has a Thursday evening option. Though I'm not a regular volunteer on Thursdays, I help from time to time. It's bigger, with more classes, more clients, and more volunteers.

The Thursday evening budget program meets at a different church, and we head there today. Not only do I know how to get to this church, but I also know how long it will take, which removes both items of uncertainty from our typical Sunday church visits.

A bit of online investigation reminds me this church is part of a denomination, one prevalent in the area. We've already visited three: *The Outlier Congregation*, *The Traditional Denominational Church*, and *The Church with a Fresh Spin*.

Their website also informs me they have one service time but two options, with the second being a simulcast feed. They name the second option but not its location. Curious.

We arrive fifteen minutes early to a packed parking lot, with some people already using their overflow spaces. Just as I'm about to veer toward one, I spot a couple of empty slots in their main lot and scoot into one.

The facility entrance I use on Thursdays is far away and, though I've never been to the sanctuary, I doubt that door is the best one to use. The main entrance, complete with a covered drop-off area, is not close either and would require more walking than I want to do in the biting wind of today's weather. Though a bright sun beckons, the conditions are far from comfortable. The closest door is a side entrance, which is where most people head.

We follow them, suspecting that once inside, we'll need to wander around to find the sanctuary. As the door closes behind us, we have two options: one flight of stairs going down and the other up. We go up, ending in a medium-sized room of undiscernible purpose. It's too large for a classroom and too small for a fellowship hall. We weave our way through it, spilling into a hallway, one lined with mail slots for member communication.

An older gentleman walks up, smiling broadly. "Should I know you? You look a little familiar."

"No," I assure him. "We're visiting today."

"Welcome!" We shake hands and exchange names.

"I sometimes help on Thursday nights with the budget program."

He smiles again. "Sometimes my wife and I help out too." Maybe we have seen each other after all.

"We have two options for the service. One is in the sanctuary," he says with a tip of his head to indicate a general direction. "It's live. The other is simulcast, and you can watch on a big screen. But they're both the same." Though he doesn't explain how to find option two, it's somewhere in the building.

We chat some more. By the time we're finished, I feel at ease, having enjoyed a pleasant connection, even though I've already forgotten his name, despite my best efforts not to. Candy and I head to the sanctuary. We take a meandering path but find it with no wrong turns or needing directions.

People stand about in the narthex, all engaged in conversation. Seeing no one available to talk to, we snake our way through the crowd toward the sanctuary. As we near, one woman aborts her conversation to greet us. She knows we're visitors and welcomes us warmly. We have a pleasant conversation, and she introduces her friend to us. By the time we make it to the sanctuary, I feel embraced and accepted, ready to immerse myself into the service. What a key difference a couple of people can make. An usher seats us and hands us bulletins.

Based on the construction, I judge this part of the facility to be about fifty or sixty years old, though it's nicely maintained. The sprawling structure has several additions, explaining our confusion on where to enter and how to reach the sanctuary.

With steep vaulted ceilings, the space is long and not wide, reminiscent of older cathedrals, though not as ostentatious, except for the impressive organ pipes on one side. An elegant oversized cross draped with a white burial cloth is the focus up front. It's flanked by two banners proclaiming, "He has risen, just as he said." On each side of the stage hangs a screen, poised to guide us through the service.

The room seats about five hundred and fills fast. No wonder they need overflow space in another part of their building, though having two services might be a better solution.

The attendees' age skews older. Candy and I are in the younger half of the crowd. Though I spot some young families, I see no one who looks college-aged and notice only a few teens. I wonder about the ages of the folks in the simulcast room. Do they skew younger?

When the service begins, we're at about 80 percent capacity. We sing two contemporary songs to the light pop accompaniment of a piano, guitar, and drums, with two vocalists. Though the male and female singers stand on the stage, the musicians are sequestered to the left, on our level in the corner. The words appear overhead on the dual screens. The pipe organ sits unused and, to my wife's delight, we never open their traditional hymnal.

Following the opening song set is a short liturgy and then a "special music" solo. Though the words appear in the bulletin, no one sings along. It's a performance, and we reward the singer with resounding applause.

As the minister calls the kids forward for the children's message, he invites the youngsters in the overflow room to join us in the main sanctuary, granting them permission to run in church. Soon they arrive, sprinting in along the side aisle, faces beaming. About twenty-five sit and anticipate what the pastor will share. He talks about trust and taps a boy for an object lesson. "Do you trust me?" The boy thinks he might. "Then turn around and when I count to three, fall backward, and I'll catch you." It takes two tries, but with the second attempt, the boy succeeds, providing a visual aid to support the minister's lesson.

After the kids return to their parents, the pastor gives the morning prayer (a traditional congregational prayer). Following it is the offertory prayer, given by a member. As the ushers receive the collection, we listen to a piano solo and fill out the friendship folders, passing them down our rows. Immediately after the offering is a second one, this one for the benevolence fund. We sing another song and hear another prayer.

The minister stands on the stage to deliver his message, separated from us by both distance and height. A gulf divides us. Sitting in the middle of the sanctuary, I'm too far back to make out any facial expressions of the preacher, so the folks in the back must have a terrible view. His message is "The Joy of Believing: Facing Our Doubts," based on the passage in John 20:19–31. It focuses on the story of Doubting Thomas.

Though Doubting Thomas becomes Believing Thomas, he's known for his former condition, not his ending state. The pastor talks about moving from hope to belief, from doubt to knowledge. The sermon is long. I grow tired and squirm. I want to take notes but jot nothing new—except that this account only appears in John.

After the message comes a closing prayer and a reprise of the special music number. This time we join in. To dismiss us, the pastor sings the benediction, something I've rarely encountered and am surprised to hear.

The service ends.

The minister stands by the main exit, acknowledging the congregation as they pass by. With hundreds of people to greet, he's on autopilot, mechanically shaking hands as we file past. Sweat beads on his forehead. He doesn't make eye contact with us and is already looking at the next person in line, as though eager to finish his ordeal.

Though I missed it, the bulletin says they have a coffee hour afterward. The minister didn't mention this from the pulpit, and nobody invites us to stay. With no one to talk to and no reason to stick around, we retrace the meandering path we took on the way in, eventually returning to our car. The service lasted ninety minutes, with the message pushing an hour.

Though the service was pleasing, it offered nothing special. Neither of us feels a reason to return. I didn't see anyone from the budget program, but at least I know about the church in case a client has questions.

Candy asks when we'll stop visiting churches so she can make her selection. I, too, sense the need to stop looking and settle down, to stop dating churches and commit, but there are a couple more I want to visit first, in expectation that my bride will like them.

Takeaway: Look for old practices at church that no longer make sense—such as your minister shaking hands with hundreds of people after every service—and offer a fresh and meaningful alternative. When you run out of space for your morning service, seek creative and low-cost solutions.

THE CHURCH THAT MEETS IN A SCHOOL
EXCITEMENT PREVAILS

I removed every church from my list that was part of a denomination. At best they would merely offer variations of what we've already experienced—and rejected. Left are three churches with intriguing implications. Perhaps one will click with Candy. We'll visit them the next three Sundays.

The first church meets in a public school building, which automatically increases my affinity with them. By renting space, they save themselves from the financial obligation of a mortgage and the maintenance stress of owning a building, one largely unused 97 percent of the time. I see them as wise stewards.

Their mission is to "glorify God by making disciples." Their vision is "to become an Acts 2 church." Though the passage begins and ends with worthy intents, the middle part may not work in our materialistic society with its consumerism mindset: holding "everything in common" and selling their possessions "to give to anyone who had need" (Acts 2:44–45, NIV). I wonder how closely they follow this example. Supporting this, they have five pillars: prayer, worship, instruction, community, and outreach.

Their service begins at ten and we plan our schedule accordingly. I'm glad for a little more pre-church time for my Sunday morning routine than what I have most Sundays.

As we head down the road, my prayer for our time there is fresh, as I'm able to avoid some phrases I fear I repeat too often. The sunny day further boosts my spirits. My expectations are high.

A black pickup truck driving next to us seems lost, making random lane changes, slowing down, and speeding up. They pass us and then we pass them. When I turn toward the school, they turn too. "Maybe we're both visiting the same place," I tell Candy with a grin. I turn again and they follow. I drive to the specified location, but there's no sign of a church. There are no cars and no people. But I spot cars in another lot, and I go around the block to get there. So does the pickup. "I hope they're not following us, because we're as lost as they are."

I pull into the parking lot with the cars. But there are no signs to confirm a church meeting will happen. Though I see people, no one is close enough to ask. A couple gets out of the black pickup. The guy looks familiar. We say "Hi" and confirm we're both looking for the same church. However, we can't verify we've found the right one until we go inside and ask. We head to the gym where the service will be, but the other couple heads in a different direction.

Inside the gym we meet another person, who also welcomes us—the third one to do so. We talk at length. Excitement permeates the place. A low, portable stage flanks one side of the gym. Stackable chairs, arrayed in three sections, will seat over two hundred. Most people are younger than us and very few are older. It's great to see young families in church, with lots of kids and teens. Aside from seniors, the only other group who might be missing is the college crowd, but there are no colleges nearby. We sit midway up in the center section. The chairs are functional, neither comfortable nor uncomfortable.

Five vertical floor-mounted banners stand next to the stage, reminding us of their five pillars. Before the service starts, more people welcome us, including our son and daughter-in-law's neighbors—the ones who told us about this church. Even though we're visitors, it's great when people recognize us.

A worship team of ten gathers on stage to begin the service, leading us in an opening song. It's upbeat like *The Church with Good Music*, perhaps more polished but without as much edge. Two guys play guitar, with a third on bass. A drummer and keyboardist round out the instrumentalists, with five more on vocals, ably led by their pastor.

After this solitary song comes a welcome, opening prayer, and greeting time. A women's quartet sings to an accompaniment track during the offering. Then we sing several more contemporary songs, all energetic and inviting. There's another prayer, and the kids leave the gym for their own activities. Though all the common elements of a church service are present, today they feel fresh, full of meaning, and exuding life. This is church as it should be—at least for me.

For his message, the pastor roams the stage, with an iPad strapped to his palm as an extension of himself. He glances at it periodically as he scrolls through his notes. After a while I forget it's there. They're in the middle of a series, "Living and Leaving a Legacy: Lessons from Malachi."

He runs through a lengthy list of stats about the significantly higher risks children face when they come from fatherless homes. It's dramatic, sadly sobering. Even more so is the reality that half of all children live in homes without their biological dads. How much better our world would be if men would stick around to live with the kids they fathered. Though a few have no choice, most do.

With this as an introduction, he pauses and prays again before reading today's text from Malachi 2:10–16. The priests in Malachi's day lead the people astray through their poor example. They divorce their wives and marry foreign women, both prohibited by the Law of Moses. In doing so they commit idolatry and adultery. This is point one: "They profane the covenant of marriage." Though there is much more to his message, neither of us catch any more points. Perhaps we'll need to come back next week to hear point two.

Regardless, he has much more to share. To leave a legacy, we need to produce godly offspring. This starts with parents and includes the Word of God. We also need to get involved in church. He sums up his message with the encouragement, "It is most rewarding to see our kids grow up to follow God." This is our chief legacy. He concludes by giving the congregation a set of challenges applicable to each life situation: parents, dads, married couples, and single adults.

As he runs through announcements, the kids return to join their parents. Today the church talks in depth about child sponsorship through Compassion International. A few members share their experiences sponsoring kids in developing countries. People can learn more after the service, even select a child to support. After an hour and a half, the service ends with a request for everyone to help pick up chairs.

More people welcome us, and we enjoy meaningful conversations with several. After a while, I walk across the now chairless gym to talk with the visitors who arrived with us. I learn they normally go to *The Rural Church*—the fourth one we visited and which I called "country fresh."

"We visited there last fall," I tell the man. "That must be why you look familiar." He nods but seems doubtful. But as we continue to share our stories, he remembers me. We had an extended conversation when we visited his church six months ago. "Your church is one of our top choices. We really liked it. We'll probably revisit it in a few months." I hope we'll see him when we do.

It's been an hour since the service ended, and the crowd has thinned, but twenty or thirty people linger to hang out. The pastor remains at the exit, talking with an attendee. We walk up and he tells us more about their church, including how they bring on new members. He isn't being presumptuous, just helpful. I appreciate the information.

I also realize this church is one of my top choices,

perhaps even moving into first place. As we discuss our experience, my bride confirms the music was good. Though she stops short of my level of enthusiasm, she doesn't dismiss them either. I suspect we'll return. I hope we do.

We have two more churches to visit. Then we will narrow down our options, and Candy will decide. Part of me wishes I had never promised her she could pick our next church. Nevertheless, I'm excited about visiting the next two churches, revisiting our top picks, and finally settling down.

Takeaway: Doing church in new ways can bring in a freshness and vitality that today's seekers want.

THE FRIENDLY CHURCH
RETIRED AND WELCOMING

This church has an innocuous name, giving no clue about who they are. But this is precisely why I didn't dismiss them. Besides judging churches by their affiliation—or more precisely applauding their lack of a denominational connection—I realize I've also begun judging churches by their websites.

This website has only four pages, five if you count the site map. The footer gives a date from four years ago. I'm not sure if that was when they created it or last edited it. It could be the last edit because all the information is static. The site displays two nature pictures and a map. It's short on information, weighing in at only four hundred words, three fourths of which are on the *About Us* page. It shares the basics and nothing more.

Their site reminds me of "An Intriguing Opportunity" from *52 Churches*, a "meditation group of self-realization fellowship" that mixed the Bible, Bhagavad Gita, and Kriya

Yoga. We skipped that "church," and I wonder if we should skip this one too. They earn a reprieve, however, when their "theology" section mentions several items harking from the Protestant Reformation. Though reeking of formality, at least my worry eases by confirming they're a Christian gathering and not a cult or made-up religion.

Based on what little I can glean from their sparse website, I suspect we'll find a traditional church mired in the past. However, I hold out hope there might be an exciting thread in their religious practices to appeal to my yearning for an intentional, spiritual community that seeks God in fresh ways. Despite this small sliver of hope, my realistic expectation is to be disappointed. Still, it's worth checking out on the off chance that they may offer what my wife seeks.

At five miles away, it should be a quick eight-minute drive. Candy suggests we leave a half hour early, and I agree, fully expecting we won't. However, we leave at the planned time. In no rush, I pray as I drive, asking God to teach us what he wants us to learn and that we can give back to the folks there.

My heart rate picks up as we pull in the drive. My thumping chest confirms my anxious insides. The parking lot has thirty to forty cars, so I know there's church and there will be a decent number of people. I breathe out in relief but am still anxious. We're fifteen minutes early and sit in the car for a few minutes before heading in.

A warm sun hits my face, balanced by a gentle breeze. Though the spring forecast is for 80 °F (27 °C) and humid with an afternoon chance of rain, there is only a hint of that now. It's an ideal morning, perfect for church. Given the weather, I'm wearing a T-shirt, shorts, and tennis shoes. I expect no one else will dress like me. I don't care. If they judge me for my attire, this is not the place for me.

As we approach the door, a smiling man in a suit rushes from the inside to open it for us. An affable fellow, he welcomes us with a sincere greeting and a hearty handshake. Men congregate in the hallway, some eyeing me as we walk by and most nodding their welcome. Some say "Hi" or shake my hand. Several thank us for visiting, and we chat with a few. Half the men wear suits and the rest, business casual. As I suspected, I'm underdressed. I'm not sure where the ladies are, but the entryway seems to be the men's domain.

A man motions to a pile of fresh rhubarb sitting on a table in a side hallway. "Help yourself," he says with a gracious gesture, "but don't wait too long because it will go quickly." His eyes twinkle. I suspect it's from his garden.

"I prefer that someone *else* have it," I say with a smirk. He misses my attempt at dry humor and thinks I'm being generous, deferring to others. The reality is I don't like rhubarb.

The building is newer, possibly built in the last ten years. It more resembles a single-story office building than a church. I like the feel. The hallway leads us to the sanctuary, a large rectangular room, about forty by sixty feet, with a flat ceiling.

The roving minister greets us by the doorway. "Welcome," he beams with a wide smile. "I'm Ron. I work here!" What an unassuming man. I immediately like him.

"Sit anywhere you want." He motions to the peopleless space. "There's plenty of room now, but we fill up fast at 9:30." I consider his words, wondering if he's serious. Realizing my confusion, he laughs. "Just joking. There will be plenty of room." Then he flits off.

"Do you see any bulletins?" Candy whispers. I glance around and shake my head. Given the tenor of everything else here, I fully expect to see an usher handing out bulletins. At the least, I think we'll see some on a table or in a literature rack. I don't. Perhaps I misjudged. Maybe this isn't a bulletin type of church after all.

We mosey on in. Though the back rows are empty, people have already laid claim to them by laying their Bibles, bulletins, and even purses on the seats. We move midway into the room before we find a place to sit. The row we pick has one odd chair. Though it's padded like the rest and matches, it also has arms. "Do you want the one with the arms or shall I sit there?" Candy asks. I shrug.

A lady behind us tells us in the nicest way possible that we can't sit there. It's a special chair for a member who needs one with arms. I nod. Then I point to the other end of the row. "Can we sit there?" She confirms we can.

With a smile she gives Candy her bulletin. "My husband will get me another." It's a simple one-page document. The front repeats all fifty words from the home page of their website, but instead of a waterfall picture, there is line art of a butterfly and flower. The back gives their order of worship, with two announcements at the bottom: there's a men's forum Tuesday morning and women's Bible study Tuesday afternoon. The times of these events confirm what

I see. This is a congregation of retirees. We may be the youngest ones here.

The service starts with a prelude, sung by five people with piano accompaniment. I'm not sure if they're a choir or a worship team. The words appear on an overhead screen. I assume it's there for us to follow along, but some people sing too. They have a hymnal and every song listed in the bulletin comes from it. However, they also display the words overhead.

Except for the responsive readings, we don't need the hymnals. Each reading has four parts: the leader, everyone, men, and women. However, it sounds like both genders read the men's and women's parts. After three songs comes the invocation, which morphs into us reciting the Lord's Prayer. I'm tentative, knowing there are variations for a few words, and I don't want to call attention to myself by saying the wrong phrase. Next is a lengthy congregational prayer and another hymn leading into the sermon.

During all this, a clipboard works its way through the four sections of chairs, distracting me from what's going on in the service as it winds its way up and down each row. On the top of the first page is a place for visitors to sign in and record their contact info. We are the first (and likely only) people to do so. Below it and on page two is a list of all the regulars. They need merely check their name. I count forty-six member families on the list, mostly couples but some singles. With ninety chairs and at about 75 percent full, most of their congregation must be present.

Today they have a guest speaker from a nearby denominational church. Given his affiliation, clues from the minister, and the style of the service, this must be a denomination church, albeit a stealth one. I'll need to apologize to Candy for dragging her here after I promised we wouldn't visit any more denomination churches and her telling me she wouldn't pick one.

The minister's text is familiar, from Daniel chapter three, about Shadrach, Meshach, and Abednego refusing to bow down to the golden monument. His delivery is smooth, but his body language is off-putting, exuding a smug distance, bordering on arrogance. The tone of his words is sincere, but his actions are too slick. Eventually I decide not to look at him and just listen. Still, I learn nothing new. By the end of his message, I've not taken a single note. I glance at Candy's notebook. Her page is blank.

The bulletin says that next are "offerings." I inwardly groan at the plural notation. However, despite what the bulletin states, they only take one. We sing two more songs, and the minister dismisses us.

The woman behind us invites us to stay for coffee and cookies. We nod yes. It's a good thing we agree, because she ushers us into the fellowship area so expectantly that I don't think we could have escaped without being rude. The woman's husband stands by the door shaking hands and talking with people as they leave. I enjoy seeing someone other than the minister doing this. It feels more real and less forced.

Though Candy and I have a few moments of awkward silence as we stand in the fellowship hall, the people give us a lot of attention. Many thank us for visiting and encourage our return with the words, "We hope you'll come back."

As we talk with the folks, we tell them we're new in the area and visiting churches. I share with several people that I saw their website and was intrigued. Each time, they smile and nod. I'm not sure if this means they're pleased their website is working or that they didn't know they had one and are being polite. Either conclusion is possible.

As the crowd thins, the minister also comes up and talks some more. His attention is nice but not needed. The congregation excels at reaching out. A second person apologizes that they had a guest speaker today and invites us back to hear their minister, who is "really good."

A third person surprises me. She says they're nondenominational. I'm shocked, so sure they were part of a denomination. I guess they can be nondenominational with a traditional vibe, just as *The Church That Meets in a School* was nondenominational with an evangelical vibe.

Even when people attempt to form a new faith gathering, they're informed by their past practices and preferences. I wonder if a nondenominational church can truly be void of denominational influences.

Curiously, the person we talk to the most and make the deepest connection with is not a member. She lives in another town and comes to this church when she visits her parents. That makes her a regular visitor. Interestingly, as we've visited churches, in many cases the person we connect with most deeply is also a visitor and not a member. This has happened too often to be coincidence.

Nevertheless, we leave feeling accepted and embraced. This is the friendliest of the churches we've visited so far and one of the few who shared food afterward. Friendly, however, isn't enough. Their services are too traditional to connect with me; their theology, too stoic; and their future, too dim. If we were retired and wanted to plug into a comfortable church with idyllic ease in a close-knit church community, this would be the ideal place.

Comfortable, however, is not our goal.

Takeaway: Know that for many visitors, your church website will be their first stop. Make sure yours is inviting, easy to understand, and clearly communicates who you are.

THE EVANGELICAL/CHARISMATIC CHURCH

CONFUSING MESSAGING

I'm excited about visiting the last church on our list—or at least the final church we intend to visit. Our plans could change, and with God, they often do.

Unlike last week, this church's website provides a lot of useful information. On their *About* page, they call themselves "an independent, charismatic fellowship." After visiting too many area churches that minimize the role of the Holy Spirit, I look forward to a church that doesn't. I'm also encouraged that they're independent, with no denominational baggage to slow them down or siphon off funds.

But their next line contradicts their claim of independence by stating they belong to a network alliance of churches. Either they're independent, or they aren't. My enthusiasm dims.

They post plenty of pictures on their website, photos of people smiling and having fun. The adults featured are mostly younger and with lots of kids, not all with white skin.

For an area with little racial diversity, a church with some cultural variation encourages me.

They offer all the programs common in church: Sunday school, nursery, youth groups, a college group, men's ministry, women's ministry, and small groups (albeit with a different label). Sunday school is concurrent with the church service, forcing both the kids and their teachers to miss the experience of community worship. Though they don't have a Sunday evening service, they do have a Wednesday night prayer meeting. I don't want a church that does what every other church does. I yearn for something different, something fresh and rooted in the mindset of the early church.

As I page through their website, I notice one conspicuous absence: the Holy Spirit. After a careful study, I see him only on the *What We Believe* page and the *Senior High* page.

Once a month high school students get together for "radical worship and times of contemplation where we wait, listen, pursue Jesus, and minister to each other in the Holy Spirit." Junior high and up may join them.

Why just once a month? Shouldn't we embrace the Holy Spirit every day?

I wonder what the Sunday service will be like. Like last week, I hope for the best while braced for disappointment, though expectation prevails. Soon I'll find out.

As we head for the church, I pray for our time there. The route is easy, but the entrance isn't marked well, and I drive past it. A long drive reveals a parking lot that is filling up and a building larger than I expected.

The church is sixteen years old and has been meeting

here for the past eleven. I assume they built the building, so it must be just over a decade old. The exterior is metal, and Candy calls it a pole barn. Though harsh, she's essentially correct.

As we head to the door, we enjoy a nice spring day with warm sunshine and a gentle breeze. Unlike last week, when I felt anxious on my approach, today I feel peace. Greeters, one outside the door and the other just inside, compete to offer us bulletins. Both are pleasant, but neither offers more than their brochure.

Inside is a bustle of people. Some give us wary smiles, but most ignore us. We weave our way through the masses toward the sanctuary. One man, smiling broadly, approaches us with intention. "Hi," he beams as we shake hands. "People call me Doc."

I share our names and ask the obvious question. "Why do people call you Doc?"

His eyes sparkle. "I used to be a doctor, but if you call me Doctor, I'll need to send you a bill."

"Well, we don't want that, Doc."

As we talk, a woman tries unsuccessfully to get his attention. Though I see this, Doc doesn't. It's not until we're walking away that I learn her mission: she wants to make sure we sign their visitor card. Eventually, she gives one to Candy, along with a pen and some brief instructions.

We sit off the middle aisle, a third of the way up. The padded chairs are comfortable, pleasing enough that I never give them another thought. There are four sections, capable of seating 280. In addition, there are a few high tables and chairs behind us.

The space is simple, but nicely finished, giving no hint on the inside of what the outside suggests. Centered in the front, positioned as high as permitted by the gently sloped ceiling, hangs a large screen. Below it is a stage, elevated by three steps. A traditional wooden pulpit sits in the center, the only dated accessory in the place. Lining the back of the stage is a series of curtains, hanging from metal rods supported by metal posts. Behind them is the hint of what might be a baptistery.

The place quickly fills, as people buzz with excitement. Kids abound, a few of them with darker skin, just as their website shows. However, I don't see any adults with the same skin color. Curious.

I also check out the bulletin. Here they call themselves evangelical, with no mention of charismatic. Though rare in my experience, it's possible to be both evangelical and charismatic, but one trait always predominates. Which one is it for this church?

I scan their list of elders and deacons. All the elders are male, as are all but one deacon. I wonder if this is by design and doubt it's by coincidence. I'm discouraged when churches place limits on how women can serve. Last, I see that the "youth band" will lead the service next Sunday. My experiences with youth leading worship have all been positive, and I wish it were happening today. Their normal worship team, however, might also be good. Soon we'll find out.

Seven people open the service, leading us in song. The worship leader also plays keyboard. Other musicians play guitar, bass guitar, drums, and piano. Two more sing backup vocals. The music feels alive. I sense God's presence. Though the song is unfamiliar to me, its message clicks. Next is a greeting and prayer. The minister reminds us that it's Memorial Day weekend, and some members are gone. Since they're at about 75 percent capacity today, they surely fill the place when everyone is in town.

The pastor also informs us it's Pentecost Sunday, fifty days after Jesus's resurrection. Today we celebrate God sending the Holy Spirit to the early church. It's fitting we're here on such an important day, even if I didn't realize it. The service will be different this Sunday, with extended music and a shorter teaching. They'll also celebrate Holy Communion, with the suggestion that through Communion we'll finish the message—whatever that means. Sunday school is on hold today.

Next is a lengthy music set, contemporary songs that resonate with me. Along the side and in the opposite front corner, kids wave flags. One is so exuberant that his flag flies off the pole. Though some kids appear to do it just for the fun of it, others connect their flags' movements with the music, worshiping God through motion. One woman also waves a flag, although stealthily. I wonder how many other adults would like to worship God in this way but are too self-conscious. I wonder the same about me.

Many adults raise their arms as we sing, physically worshiping God. For the first time in eighteen churches, this is the accepted norm. Most of the churches we visited were stoic in their worship and for those who weren't, raising hands was an anomaly. Today, it feels natural. I join them, happy to do so.

A lengthy list of announcements follows. The pastor says they don't meet for Wednesday prayer in the summer. I'm dismayed. Does this imply it's okay to take a break from prayer when other activities are more pressing? I'm so preoccupied by this that I miss the rest of the announcements.

The minister starts his "short message," again saying we will finish it when we take the Lord's Supper. This perplexes me. Is he speaking figuratively, or will this Communion celebration differ from my other experiences, allowing us the opportunity to complete his message verbally as we partake? I'm excited at the prospect and worried over the unknown.

He reads John 12:27–33 but starts teaching at verse 20. I jot down several thoughts: Greeks are present, which is most unusual; they approach Philip, not Jesus; Philip goes to Andrew and, together, they bring the Greeks to Jesus; the door opens to Gentiles, but some people will never believe. Though these are interesting, the teaching ends without me grasping a main point or takeaway.

"By taking Communion with your family," he says, "we take a stand and complete the message." I'm still confused. Though he makes no invitation for nonmembers to partake, Doc was thoughtful enough to tell us we could. Without his approval, I would have sat in isolation while everyone else took part. *Thanks, Doc.*

With seven stations, each one staffed by an elder or deacon, we have options. People go forward as families. Most linger after they take the Communion elements, sometimes in conversation, other times in prayer. After observing the process, we get in line.

As it works out, we're among the last to reach the front. The man holds out a plate with broken crackers. We each take one, and he says something. Candy and I look at each other, wondering what to do. As he reaches for the tray with small cups of juice, we shove the pieces of cracker in our mouths. With a nod, we pick up the juice and drink it. Without another word, he accepts our empty cups, and we sit down. Did I miss something? Were we supposed to interact with him? Was he supposed to interact with us? Not only did we miss the community others enjoyed, but the process so distracted me that I missed the meaning of Communion. *Forgive me, Lord Jesus.*

After this, the minister recognizes a deacon and elder whose terms are ending; we applaud their service. He begins to offer the benediction when someone stops him. "Oh yeah, I almost forgot the offering—again. You'd think we didn't need money."

He launches into a lengthy discourse on giving, their budget shortfall, their plans, and the need to give. He claims he never talks this long about money, but I wonder who he's trying to convince. Then he talks about it some more. During this time, people wait patiently at the front of each of the five aisles, holding offering baskets. He forgets they're standing there and finally notices them, permitting them to collect the offering. As the basket goes by, I spot only a few bills in the bottom. Candy drops in our visitor card, with the pen clipped to it.

As another addendum, the minister asks some church leaders to come up after the service to pray for him and his upcoming trip to Africa. Then the service ends.

We gather our things with intentional deliberation, giving time for the people sitting nearby to talk to us. But no one does. No one looks our way. I hope for someone to approach us, but no one does. As we file out, one deacon asks if this is our first time there. When we confirm it is, he asks if we have questions. I do, but none come to mind until later. I tell him "No." The conversation ends.

Doc makes his way to us, thanking us for visiting and inviting us back. He introduces us to some nearby people, but our interaction is nothing more than a handshake or head nod. Then we repeat the process in how we entered, weaving our way between people who barely know we're there.

We return to our car, ninety minutes after we arrived. Before I can ask, Candy shares her opinion. "The music was safe, and they were off-key sometimes."

I groan. "I liked the music and thought it was some of the best we've encountered." Though a handful of other churches are better, I ignore that fact for now. "I felt God's presence, like I haven't felt it at church for a long time."

"That could be," my wife responds, "but the music was still safe and off-key." She's probably right.

What we agree on is the pastor's awkwardness. The congregation seems to accept his quirky communication traits, but I know they would grate on me. And aside from Doc, they weren't at all friendly. Making meaningful connections there would be hard. I don't feel up to the challenge.

Despite some elements I really liked and an imperative desire for this church to click with me, they fell short. As I feared, I'm disappointed. Candy eliminates them from further consideration, so I do too. We'll get home around noon. I wonder what's for lunch.

Takeaway: Make sure your church website sends a clear and consistent message about who you are and what you value.

I later email the church asking if adults are welcome at the monthly time when high schoolers radically worship God and listen to the Holy Spirit. I'd like to join them. No one responds. I could try calling them, but by now I've given up on the idea.

STILL GOOD BUT FALLING SHORT
RETURNING TO THE RURAL CHURCH

At this point we've considered nineteen churches. We could have easily gone to scores more—stretching our search out for several more months—but it's time to decide. Some options will remain unexplored.

Part of me senses this is unfair. I've summarily dismissed some potentially viable options based entirely on their name. I didn't even bother to make an in-person visit before rejecting them. In most cases I didn't even take the time to look at their website. The ones I've excluded all have one thing in common: their stodgy name clearly communicates they're part of a denomination.

Yes, I'm down on denominations. As I say often: "Denominations are the antithesis of the Christian unity Jesus prayed for." And I'm a huge proponent of Christians and their churches getting along. Denominations do the opposite. They divide us and wall us off from other

Christians for no good reason. It's unbiblical, opposing the desire of Jesus that we would live as one (John 17:20–23).

While denominations provide some benefit, such as local church oversight, a pooling of resources, and group buying power, the price to do so is too high. There are additional layers of bureaucracy, which leads to inaction, perpetuating the status quo, and maintaining the denomination as an institution. Many people work for denominations full time, dedicated to these tasks, when they could better serve at the local level, to grow Jesus's church by sharing the Word and making disciples. Too often, the denominational focus is on self-preservation more than changing lives.

Another concern is that the cost to support the denominational structure siphons off money from local congregations and local needs to support a machine that seeks to control what happens at the local level. For what it costs, they add little to the cause of Jesus. Yes, denominations send missionaries, plant churches, and respond to crises. But local churches can do this too. While denominations may react more quickly to crises, local churches can be more effective.

Yes, we visited denomination churches. Some of the nineteen have denominational connections. But now I wonder why we considered them.

Personally, I seek community at church. True, meaningful, deep, spiritual community. Music and message are secondary. Beyond that, I want to go to a church in my community, where at least some of my neighbors attend. Now I add to my list that I want them to be independent, not part of a denomination.

Initially Candy said she wanted a church with excellent

music, one that isn't afraid to speak biblical truth—even if it puts their tax-exempt status at risk. For her, *The Nonconventional Church* remains her top pick, while she concedes that *The Rural Church* is a consideration, along with *The Church that Meets in a School.*

We'll make repeat visits to these churches.

Candy will make the final decision. My role is advisory.

In considering my four requirements, *The Rural Church* meets only one. When we were there, we experienced great community and made several connections. However, they aren't in our community, no neighbors attend there, and they're part of a denomination. As a bonus, our son and daughter-in-law plan to switch to this church. This would allow the four of us to be part of the same church community. Though the locations of some churches would be central for us and all four of our kids, this one is too far away for our daughter and son-in-law.

I look forward to reconnecting with the people we met before and spending time in this friendly environment. I also know that with two services, our chance of seeing the folks we met last fall is less likely. We plan to meet our son and daughter-in-law there.

It's a nice spring day, warm with plenty of sunshine. It's hard to believe it's been nine months since our first visit. Interestingly, the weather is about the same now as it was then. Full of expectation, perhaps too much, we hop in our car and head off, saying a prayer as we go. The trip, at 6.2

miles, is quick. Once we leave our subdivision, we head straight south, encountering minimal traffic, just two stop signs, and making no turns. It takes eight minutes.

We pull into their lot about ten minutes before the second service should begin. The small lot in front is mostly full, and we take one of the few remaining spots. We don't see our son's car. Though they could have parked in the other lot, we assume they aren't here yet. I want to get inside to look for them.

In the parking lot I spot a man we met during our first visit. He and his wife spent a lot of time with us after the service. I instantly connected with him and his family. Since then, I've seen him one other time, yesterday at our garage sale. It was our daughter-in-law who first recognized his wife, but soon we all remembered each other and our time together some nine months ago. We re-exchanged names. Interestingly, his brother lives near our house but goes to a different church.

It's wonderful to see someone we know before we even get inside. We talk for a few minutes and then head for the entrance. We encounter the same mass of people as last time, though this time a few of them say "Hi" or nod a greeting. I don't see our son and daughter-in-law.

Candy and I sit toward the back of the sanctuary, one of the few spots left for four people. The stage is distant, and the space doesn't feel as open as I remember. We're too far back for my liking.

The senior pastor's wife comes up to welcome us, not sure if she should know us or not. We have a brief exchange. Soon our kids arrive. The service is about to start.

The worship team gathers on the stage, forming a circle to pray first. I so like this, with the example they set and the priority they portray. The opening song is a familiar one, which normally is upbeat and uplifting. Though the instrumentation is good, the vocals fall short. What should draw us in pushes us away as the words plod along like a funeral dirge.

My wife criticized the music on our first visit. Though I knew it wasn't the best, it didn't detract from my worship then. Today it does. By the time they make it to the chorus, the song leader mostly finds his place, easing into a somewhat accessible tone. Still, he falls far short of how powerful this song normally sounds.

After the opening number, the youth pastor gets up and implores everyone to fill out the yellow cards in our bulletins. "We need these to report numbers to our bosses," he says. I groan at the reminder they're part of a denomination, one that tracks their church's attendance.

He shares two announcements, the first about their Annual Church Conference, another reminder of their denomination's practices and their formal governance. The early church didn't vote on overtures or elect leaders. Though this is the democratic way, it lacks biblical support. Over the years, I've had my fill of church committees, meetings, and elections.

Set politics aside. Put God first.

The other announcement is about an upcoming children's dedication. Interested parents must attend a class first. This church practices believer's baptism for adults and children's dedication for kids.

Then we sing some more. After a bit, the pastor invites people to come forward to the altar to pray, while the rest of us sing. I don't see an altar, and I'm not sure what he means, but people come forward, some in expectation while others plod. They kneel on the steps of the stage to pray. When the song ends, they retreat to their seats.

An opening video introduces their new series, "Dealing with Fear." Again, I'm impressed that a church this size (last Sunday's attendance was 342) produces videos for their services. Last time they showed two.

The sermon title is "Fear of Failure." The senior pastor teaches today. "We fear God," he says, "or we fear everything else." A related reoccurring theme is risk. "Not taking risks will ultimately lead to failure."

The pastor shares, at length, his own journey of failures, of risks taken and risks avoided. Last time he also used personal anecdotes to introduce the message. I still remember what he shared then. I wonder if self-disclosure is his normal practice.

Like last time, I fill my journal with a page of notes, right down to the last line. Today, God has a message for me. I've become risk averse for what matters most. In recent months, the Holy Spirit has nudged me to act at various times. But I didn't. Though I don't know the outcome, I must take the risk anyway.

"Failure is part of our success," he says to conclude his message. To wrap up, the pastor leads the congregation in a prayer of commitment. It's not a prayer of rededication and certainly not one of salvation. I miss the intended purpose. Maybe it is for us to confront our fears and take risks.

He says the closing prayer, they take the offering, and we sing a final song, a mash-up of an old hymn and modern choruses. Despite the song leader, the overall result is pleasing. All the songs were great. I expect they'll reverberate in my mind for the next several days. The instrumentation added to the experience, but the vocals were the weak link. Hopefully, he just had an off day.

Afterward I look for the people we met before but don't see any of them, not even the couple we reconnected with when we were both visiting *The Church That Meets in a School*. I try to make eye contact with others as they file out, but I'm unsuccessful.

Resigned for no after church interaction, the four of us discuss lunch. Before we leave, I use the restroom. When I return, the senior pastor is talking with the rest of my family. He greets me by name. I assume someone prompted him, but they didn't. He also remembers Candy's name and where our son and daughter-in-law are building their house, noting it's near completion. He has an amazing memory, and we enjoy a meaningful conversation. We leave feeling content.

We debrief at lunch.

All agree the worship leader struggled today with his opening song. It was painful and hard to overlook. Next month they'll have a newcomers' lunch. We discuss going, though we stop short of committing. They also have a Wednesday midweek meeting that starts at 6 p.m. with food, followed by classes for all ages. I'd like to go to share a meal and meet people, but the class options don't interest me.

The thing that most endears me to this church is their

after-church interaction at our first visit. Then, the pastor told the congregation to spend their first three minutes after the service getting to know someone new. They did, and we benefited. I assumed this was their norm. Today he didn't make any such announcement, and no one bothered. I had lofty expectations for community and was disappointed, despite them being friendlier than most churches.

Our daughter-in-law grew up in this denomination and feels quite at home there. Her enthusiasm remains. As for our son and me, our interest has waned. Discouraged, I move this church down my list to the third spot. For Candy it was already there. We'll need to return a few more times to be sure, but right now, I suspect this is not our next church home.

We make our third visit the following week, again with our kids. It's great for us to be in church together. What we experience this time is an average of our two prior visits: not as good as the first but better than the second.

I sign Candy and I up to go to their newcomers' picnic. I'd like to check out their Wednesday evening meeting, too, but it's wrapping up for the summer. By the time it resumes in the fall, as well as their life groups, we'll have made our church selection. But we'll need to do so without experiencing these two options.

A month later we make our fourth visit to this church. On our quick drive, we pray for our time there. I have mixed feelings. Though we enjoy engaging conversations each Sunday, we seldom reconnect with those folks on subsequent visits. The church is big enough to make forming recurring community a challenge, and having two services hinders that even more.

I bypass the closest drive and head to the bigger parking lot on the other side of their facility. We've never gone in these doors before, but they are the main entrance and open right into the sanctuary. This sure beats the roundabout path we've taken on prior weeks.

Some people, a few who look familiar, nod a greeting or say "Hello," but their outreach is nothing more than an acknowledgment. But at least they notice us. As we move forward into the sanctuary, one woman approaches us with intention. We met her and her husband on our first visit and we enjoyed getting to know them. They were also the couple we were surprised to see at our visit to *The Church That Meets in a School*.

I'm glad to see her but can't remember her name. Realizing I won't recall it until too late, I apologize and ask her to remind me.

"Janet," she says.

"We were here a couple weeks ago and looked for you, but we didn't see you." My intention is to communicate interest, but I may have sounded accusatory. She doesn't, however, take offense.

"We usually go to the first service and hang out until the second one starts."

"And we've always gone to the second one. I'm glad we could see you today." Her husband stands nearby but talks with another group. She and I struggle over what to say. Even though Candy joins us, our words remain awkward as we grapple with conversation.

"It was really great to see you," I say with all sincerity, despite our uncomfortable exchange. "I think we're going to find our seats now . . . I hope you have a great afternoon."

The countdown timer says 4:12, but I doubt they'll start then. But with a minute remaining the worship team gathers on stage to pray, and when the time hits zero, the music begins. The associate pastor, flanked by eight others—musicians and vocalists—leads us in song. Though under-amplified, his confident voice and engaging stage persona is ideal to lead us. He ably led the worship music on our first visit, drawing us into the service. The bulletin says he's the "Pastor of Worship and Youth," but the website gives his title as "Pastor of Volunteer Services, Operations and Events."

On our second and third visit they had another worship leader who struggled. One Sunday, his leading was especially difficult to follow. Though the website lists him as the "Sunday Worship Leader," the bulletin doesn't mention him.

The service proceeds as usual, and soon it's time for the sermon. Though the bulletin lists another person as the "Teaching Pastor," we've only heard the lead pastor speak. He's a good teacher, and I always end up with a page of notes. Though I rarely learn much that's new, the Holy Spirit uses his words to provoke other insights. Some of his teaching today gives me ideas for a book I'm writing.

We wrap up with Communion, our first time at this church. The pastor clearly communicates that nonmembers who have a relationship with Jesus may participate. I appreciate knowing their policy on this. We file up to receive the bread and the juice, taking them back to our seats to eat them in unison. Though consuming them as a congregation is what I experienced most of my life, it has been several years since I've done it this way. There's a comfortable rhythm of taking the communion elements together, as though we're demonstrating harmony and proclaiming agreement.

The service lasts longer than we expect, and we need to scoot out to meet friends for lunch. We'll be late. But we'll also return in a few hours for the newcomers' picnic.

With threatening skies and rain looming, our picnic in the park relocates to the Kids Center at the church. There are many more people than I expected. As I scan the crowd, I wonder who are regulars and who are newcomers. We mingle awkwardly for a few minutes. Then the pastor begins. He welcomes us and prays for the meal: grilled hamburgers and hot dogs, chips, veggies, lemonade, and desserts.

Candy and I sit, and our son and daughter-in-law join us. For a while we are alone, but eventually another couple come up. They're members, and we met them on our first visit. As the meal wraps up, the lead pastor again stands, telling us about the church: there's no pressure to become members, but they do want us to become involved. Their programs are finished for the summer and will resume in the fall. They'll also add a third Sunday service in a few months but haven't worked out the details.

He stresses how they want to make a difference in their community. But we aren't part of their community. I want to make a difference in *my* community, not someone else's. I want to go to church in my neighborhood, with my neighbors.

Though there's excitement in attending a growing church, the idea of three services is disconcerting. Even with two, it's easy to miss folks. Three will make it even harder. Though he asserts he doesn't want to make us uncomfortable, he asks us to stand and introduce ourselves to the group, one representative from each family. I groan as I mentally prepare to answer his four questions: our names, what we like about the church, how long we've been attending, and how we heard about them.

Our table goes first, so my agony is soon over. As the introductions move from table to table, I realize members have strategically interspersed themselves with newcomers at each table. Though the "what we like about the church" part feels a bit too self-serving, it's encouraging to learn the story of how each family ended up here.

To wrap up, they pass out cards to collect our contact information, along with what our next steps are and where we'd like to serve. Though the pastor stresses there's no obligation or expectation, I feel pressure. I fill out the top part, but they collect the cards before I figure out what to put on the rest. Candy later tells me she followed my example. I wonder if they'll contact us.

On the drive home, we discuss this church. On the plus side, they don't push membership, they are friendly, and community exists. The messages are thought-provoking, and the music was engaging at two of our four visits. They are a growing church, with lots of kids. Their future is bright. Our son and daughter-in-law plan to go there.

On the negative side, their community is not our community, none of our neighbors go there, and they're larger than I'd like. Aside from the Sunday morning service, I'm not sure how I could plug in or where I could serve. Also, they're part of a denomination and are too far away for our daughter and son-in-law to consider.

Though they could become our church family, I don't think we'll give them the chance. We may visit occasionally with family but will pick another church as our home. We still have *The Church That Meets in a School* and *The Nonconventional Church* to consider.

Takeaway: Have a plan to turn visitors into regular attendees and work your plan.

A DIFFERENT EXPERIENCE

RETURNING TO THE CHURCH THAT MEETS IN A SCHOOL

When I wake up on Sunday morning, I have little interest in going to church. I feel no need. We enjoyed a fulfilling spiritual experience yesterday at a wedding and reception. Today's effort will surely pale in contrast. Yes, it could be a spiritual experience. We may enjoy meaningful community; but I doubt it will be a celebration like we had last night.

Why can't church be more like a wedding, celebrating God in real community? I think that's how it should be. And I think that's what our Lord wants.

Before getting out of bed, I ask God to prepare me for the day ahead. Though my prayer is sincere, it's unfocused. I'm still basking in the afterglow of hanging out with friends last night.

Our son and daughter-in-law are staying with us for a time while they're between homes. We hop in the car to visit *The Church That Meets in a School*, the first time for our kids and a return trip for Candy and me. I'm excited about the four of us going together. I also invited our daughter and her family.

As we drive, we talk about the church, what we know about it and a bit of Candy's and my experience on our first visit. My anticipation builds, but I also forget to pray for our time there.

We had trouble finding it on our first visit. Though I avoid making that same mistake today, I still can't find the path to take us straight to their parking lot. This time I overshoot my destination and need to backtrack. We arrive six minutes early.

A man I met on our first visit waves to us. It's nice to be noticed. "Today will not be a typical service." His smile hints at a surprise. When I ask for details, he dismisses me. "You'll need to go inside to find out." *If he tells us, is he afraid we'll leave?* Worry builds in my gut.

Wary, we head inside. Today the gym is not set up for a church service. It's arrayed cafeteria style. "Sit anywhere," someone says. "We're having a volunteer appreciation breakfast." I assume the breakfast is wrapping up and a service of some sort will soon start. I'm wrong. It's the breakfast that's about to begin.

Though I applaud their flexibility in how they spend time together on Sunday morning, I'm uneasy. I feel we're imposing on a private gathering. We picked the wrong Sunday to visit. The pastor stands to explain the situation, inviting all to share in the meal. Just as he's about to pray for the food, the rest of our family arrives, and Candy waves them over. We have room saved for them at our table.

Each of us has already eaten breakfast, but we decide to be social and eat again. Our daughter-in-law asks, "If the breakfast is for volunteers, who's making it?" That's a good question. As we wait in line for our food, we meet a few more people, and as we eat, more stop by. Our son and daughter-in-law's future neighbors soon join us. As the meal wraps up, the pastor shifts into part two of the morning's activities.

He calls up six people for volunteer interviews. Though he planned this and has questions prepared, he struggles at interviewing, and the volunteers squirm. I suspect his goal is to show everyone how easy it is to volunteer and how rewarding it is. This, however, doesn't happen. The hours the volunteers invest add up, and they share how they struggled along the way. The result is a lesson in persevering.

Next, he talks about the 80-20 rule, where 20 percent of the people do 80 percent of the work. Attempting to prove this church is the exception, he asks volunteers to stand as he calls their name or area of service. In the end, over 20 percent are standing, but not much more.

He talks about the importance of joining their church, of committing and becoming members. This, he implies, is a necessary part of our faith journey. I groan. Then, once we become members, we shouldn't expect to be served but to seek ways to serve.

Throughout his discourse we have trouble hearing, this is partly because people around us don't care. They're engaged in personal conversations and laughter. Even more so, the portable PA system they're using isn't loud enough, and what we do hear is muffled. It's hard to connect with his message.

Afterward we help clean up and talk with more people. Unfortunately, the cleanup effort pre-empts community, so our interactions are cut short. Still, we meet more people and try to remember their names.

As we head outside, I sense we're all discouraged. I try to be positive. "I guess we'll need to come back again to experience a typical service." Based on their lack of response, I'm not sure anyone wants to.

I feel defeated. Once again, our second visit to one of our top churches was not as good as our first. Should we stop trying? Staying home is easier. Though I know I can't, that's how I feel.

Later I look at their weekly newsletter. Listed first is their recent giving. Is money what's most important to them? Donations are up for May after being down for April. I don't know how they're doing for the year, but I see they have $100,000 in their building fund. An arrow pierces my heart; it's hard to breathe.

Why do churches think they have to have a building?

A building is a drain on resources and limits future flexibility. This church wants to become an Acts 2 church, but the early church didn't own a building. They met in people's homes or public places. Why doesn't anyone see this?

My spirits lift when I see a church picnic scheduled next week. This could be a time of meaningful community and the chance to meet more people. However, they don't give details. It doesn't say potluck, so I assume that "bring a dish to pass" is not part of the plan. It also doesn't say "cookout" so I assume they will not grill anything for us. I guess picnic means to pack a lunch for your family, but that's far from the ideal of sharing everything as mentioned in Acts 2:42–47. I hate going to social events when I don't know what to expect. I go online to look for more details about the church picnic. Aside from giving dates of other ones, there's no clarification.

On their "staff and board" page, I scan their list of deacons; all are men. Likewise, their two staff members are male. I suspect this church doesn't permit women in leadership roles. *Have we stumbled into a conservative church in disguise?* I search every page of their website for answers but find no clues.

I do, however, find other information online. What I read unsettles me. Under "next steps," they say to attend church regularly, read the Bible, and pray throughout the day. I agree wholeheartedly with the last two items. While the principle of meeting together is biblical, today's practice of doing it for one hour each Sunday morning—as their website states—is far different from the practice of the early church.

However, the bad part is their "essential steps": to "get baptized," "give regularly," and "become a member." My interest sinks lower at each one. Baptism is important, but I don't see it as essential when I read the Bible. Doctrinal differences over baptism have so divided Jesus's church that I don't even want to think about it. Yes, Jesus did tell us to make disciples and baptize them (Matthew 28:19–20), but baptism wasn't an essential step to the criminal crucified next to Jesus (Luke 23:39–43).

Next is to give money to them regularly. The New Testament doesn't command us to give to the local church and the only times it mentions tithing is in reference to the Old Testament practices, which Jesus fulfilled. Giving to church is an option for how we can be stewards of the money God has entrusted us with, but it certainly isn't an *essential step*. While we need to give and be generous, it's unbiblical to insist this must be to a local church.

Last is membership. Church membership did not exist in the early church. It isn't in the Bible. It's something we made up along the way. Membership divides us. It splits followers of Jesus into two groups, those inside the institution and those outside—something organized religion has done throughout the centuries, much to its shame. Jesus is inclusive. He doesn't seek members. He wants followers.

Membership implies privileges. Whenever we become members of an organization, church included, it suggests benefits. We become members for what we will get: for a reward, to be served, and to receive. Membership is part of our consumerism mentality, which has no place in church. Church is about giving of ourselves and serving others, not the opposite.

I also scan their "what we believe" page. It's extensive, spouting a detailed discourse of nine articles, using words such as anthropology, sanctification, soteriology, ecclesiology, and eschatology. I've never heard some of these words. Jesus said we're to come to him like little children, but their intellectual theology would make that impossible. Why do people want to hinder our approach to God with their intellectual constructs?

I'm so worked up over all this that I don't want to go back. Once again. I'm reminded that today's church has no place for me. I'd drop out if not for my wife. Yes, I desire to be part of a vibrant spiritual community, but the poor substitute we find on Sunday mornings is not what I seek.

So as far as this church is concerned, how do I react? I want to go to the picnic, assuming I can find out their format. I'm open to visit again. If either of our kids and their families go here, I'm willing to go too. But I'm not willing to follow their "essential steps." I will never again be a member of a church and, unless God directs otherwise, I'll support other kingdom causes that more wisely use the money God has appointed me steward over.

I'm so discouraged. Does that leave *The Nonconventional Church* as our only remaining contender? What if my second visit to that church is likewise disheartening?

After a week to contemplate this, I'm no less worked up. If anything, I'm even less interested in going a third time, but that's exactly what our plan is for Sunday. Our son and daughter-in-law can't join us. I invite our daughter and son-in-law, but they don't respond. However, on Sunday, our daughter texts her mom that they'll join us.

For the first time in three tries, I drive straight to their parking lot with no wrong turns or wasted effort. It doesn't seem as full as last week. At the door, walking in just ahead of us, we see a friend from where we used to live. She's also visiting.

The greeter asks our names and repeats them with care, implanting them in his mind. He doesn't look familiar, but he recognizes us. He saw us last Sunday and apologizes for not talking to us then, but he was cooking the food for the volunteer appreciation breakfast. As I take in all this information, I forget his name.

In the hallway is a table selling desserts as a mission trip fundraiser. I wonder what Jesus thinks about them selling things at church. If he were here in person, would he make a whip to drive them away and upend their table? I'd like to see that. Though their enterprise is for a noble cause, it also detracts from worship. At another table, a woman dispenses information, but I don't bother to find out what.

The gym is configured for a church service, just like on our first visit. There is a bustle of activity, with most people clustered in groups, engaged in conversation. Only a few people sit. I spot two of our son and daughter-in-law's future neighbors, at least the husbands, standing next to the sound booth. They see me, and we wave. I head in their direction, but Candy spots their wives and wants to talk with them. That group seems easier to join, so I stick with my bride and the four of us have an enjoyable conversation. By the time we finish, the guys are no longer available. I look around for some of the other people we've met in the past, but I don't see anyone who looks familiar. With no one else to talk to, we sit.

It takes our daughter and son-in-law more time than they expected to deal with nursery, so by the time they join us, the service has already begun. The format is the same as the first time, an opening song, followed by announcements, which drag on for far too long. I, however, stop listening after his first one: they've canceled the picnic because of predicted rain, bolstered by the weather radar that shows storm clouds closing in. Though I'd dismissed attending the picnic, I'm disappointed they canceled it.

I tune back in when he mentions he hangs out at a local coffee shop on Thursdays and Fridays. He gives the hours and invites us to stop by if we have questions or want to talk. I really like this approach and him being accessible in public places. This is also practical since he doesn't have a church office.

The minister mentions how important membership is and encourages joining their church, which segues into a testimony from one of their new members. A young woman stands to share her story. She grew up attending a nearby Baptist church and "got saved" at the early age of four. Later she mentions the college she attended, self-described as a "nationally recognized Baptist institution." At its mention, many in the congregation cheer. Surely this is a Baptist church in disguise or a gathering of Baptist expats. I don't belong here. When she finishes sharing, the crowd applauds.

A prayer for her and other congregational needs follows. Then they take an offering. Though many people sit in front of us, only one donation lies in the plate as it passes by. During this time, a woman plays guitar and sings. The tune is familiar, but the words are in another language. "This reminds me of speaking in tongues," I whisper to Candy. "We need an interpreter."

She scowls back. "It's Spanish."

"Doesn't the same principle apply?"

She ignores me.

When the song ends, people clap.

The minister stands, telling us the words were in Spanish. When he gives the English title, some lyrics come to mind.

Next, we celebrate four high school graduates, who uncomfortably share their names, school, and plans. The staff person in charge of the youth group gives them a Bible, and the congregation applauds. There's been a lot of clapping today, but each time it's directed at people and not God.

This all takes about thirty minutes. Now the worship team comes back and leads us in a song set, lasting another twenty. Their instruments and sound are contemporary. They even weave in one hymn.

The minister starts a new series on physical touch. He'll share four stories where Jesus reaches out to touch someone. His text today is Matthew 8:1–3, about Jesus touching and healing the leprous man. This week he doesn't use an iPad but places his notes on the podium.

He spends much of his time imagining what this man's life might have been like, both before and after becoming a leper. Jesus was likely the only person to touch him since the man contracted the contagious disease.

To wrap up, the preacher says we all have a disease; it is sin. Jesus is the cure. The preacher also encourages us to have compassion toward others, like Jesus did. And we need to care for those around us.

He concludes his message, the same as the last two

times, with a request for everyone to help pick up. Unfortunately, the people who immediately comply impede those who seek interaction. As we talk with the couple sitting next to us, others worm between us to grab our chairs, even when we still have things sitting on them. They act irritated with us, just as I am with them. We each have an agenda and are in each other's way.

Even so, this is a friendly church. We've met many people in our three visits but have only seen a few of them a second time. The church is big enough that it's hard to form meaningful connections. It's also big enough that several people have asked if we're visitors or members.

This church is too big and too conservative for me. Despite many positive elements, the negatives outweigh them. Candy agrees.

Only *The Nonconventional Church* remains.

Takeaway: Are the things your church stresses the things that matter most to God?

LAST ONE STANDING

RETURNING TO THE NONCONVENTIONAL CHURCH

O n Sunday, I'm both excited and apprehensive. I'm looking forward to finally picking a church, that our journey will soon end. Yet I'm also hesitant. I haven't fully embraced this church, *The Nonconventional Church*, which effectively locked us out on our first attempt to visit.

On the plus side, they don't have the financial obligation of owning a building or of payroll (that I'm aware of). They're less like today's church and more like the early church, at least more like it than any others we've visited, though they still have a way to go. They may break from societal conventions in other of their church practices as well. Of course, I don't yet know this, but I'm hopeful.

Yet on the negative side, they're not in our community, not even close, and none of our neighbors attend there. These two things are important to me. Yes, we know people who go there—Candy, much more so than I—yet none of

them live near us. Once again, we would leave our neighborhood to go to church in someone else's. I don't want to
do that.

As we head to church, my prayer is more intentional,
more imperative than on many other Sundays. I break from
the repetition of words that so easily overtake me each
week. I ask God for a fresh perspective, and for a good attitude toward this church and the people we'll meet.

The church is about eight miles away and the drive takes
sixteen minutes. Our GPS calculates the quickest route, a
zigzag pattern of right turns, followed each time by a left.
With this route, we overshoot our destination and need to
backtrack a bit, but it's the quickest path.

We don't know if we are early or late. A few days ago, I
asked my friend who goes there if church is at ten. She hesi-
tated. "No, I think it's at 10:30." She paused again. "Yes, it's
10:30. There's no Sunday School in the summer." She
seemed unsure enough that I checked online. Their
Facebook page says it starts at 10:00.

I'm willing to follow my friend's timing, willing to risk
arriving a half hour late. Candy wants to err on the other
side, risking getting there a half hour early. We don't leave as
soon as she wants. If they do indeed start at 10, we'll be late.

We're the tenth car in the parking lot. I'm still not sure
if we're early or late. We head toward the door we went in
last time. Then it was a travel agency, now it's an
accounting firm. Recalling our first visit when we couldn't
find an unlocked entrance, I hope this door is still the
right one.

The knob turns, and we walk inside. Music, emanating

from the basement, confronts us. I sigh. We're late. I want to flee.

Candy hesitates too. She ignores my chivalrous gesture for her to go first. After a moment, we head down the stairs together, side by side. At the bottom, we turn left, walking down the hall toward the light and sound. A dozen people stand in the front, playing and singing, with fewer who are seated. At first, I think we've joined a lightly attended church service already in progress, but I realize we've walked in on a rehearsal.

There are two things Candy wants in a church: excellence in music and a willingness to speak out on social issues. Their music, though sincere and heartfelt, falls short. Yes, this is practice, but how much better can it get in twenty minutes? I don't think it's an issue of talent as much as not melding as one. There are two percussionists, a pair on sax, three on guitar, a keyboardist, and four vocalists.

Candy knows some ladies who are sitting. They stand to greet us. We try to talk but the music is too loud to allow for comfortable conversation. Eventually we give up.

One of the guitarists spots us and nods. During a break in their practice, he comes over to chat. Candy used to work with him and knows him best of anyone there. It's good to connect, for someone to notice our presence.

They resume their rehearsal, this time not as loudly. Others wander in, and we talk with a few of them. They offer us coffee, but Candy brought her own, and I don't imbibe. Then one elder hollers, "The service will start in two minutes."

A man rushes in. "Sorry I'm late," he tells a group

hovered around the soundboard. He hands them a back-pack, and they descend upon it, pulling out a laptop and cables. They need his computer to run the slides for the service. The man is their teaching elder, the closest they have to a pastor. He was sick the last time we were here, and this is the first time I see him.

Soon the service starts. The first song is familiar, and we sing along. Many people raise their hands in a physical display of worship. This has been so lacking at most of the churches we've visited, that when I do it now, it feels foreign —yet at the same time, good. In a space next to the hall we worship in, a group of young girls dance with gentle, elegant movement. Later I see a group of boys in back with their version of dance. It's more physical, almost rowdy, bordering on anarchy. I smile. Both groups offer their expression of worship to God through motion.

We continue singing, but the rest of the songs aren't familiar to me. I stumble often, glad no one can hear my mere whisper. After a few songs, a slide announces the offering will occur during the next number. As we sing, people walk forward to drop their monetary gifts into a box that sits on the floor in front of the lectern. We sing some more, wrapping up after twenty-five minutes by singing an old-time hymn accompanied by their contempo-rary instruments. Then one of their members stands and calls the kids for children's church. The kids rush out in excitement.

The minister stands, pauses, and then asks for someone to pray for him. I'm not sure if this is a special request for today or a normal practice. One man comes forward. He places his hand on the preacher's back and prays for him and our service.

Still the preacher is not ready. He says the last song has wrecked him emotionally. I've already forgotten it. But then, music isn't my thing.

Finally, he's ready to start. This week he's talking about a social issue. I groan inwardly. But I realize this is what Candy wants: a pastor willing to speak out on social issues. This all but guarantees she'll pick this church. Of course, she presumes he'll agree with her point of view.

He's a gifted speaker, easy to listen to and humble, not calling attention to himself, as too many accomplished preachers do. He has prepared his message well, with careful study and including thoughtful insights.

Yet given his topic, after an hour I'm ready for his sermon to end. It's an emotional issue, and I'm wearied at the effort I've put forth to consider his proclamations. Some I agree with but not all. A few stop short of reaching the conclusions I would make.

When he finishes speaking, one of their elders stands to give the benediction. The service is over.

Afterward friends come up to talk. They're all people Candy knows. I work hard to remember names and faces. I'm sure we'll be back, so I better learn who these folks are. We talk for another half hour, but in all this, no one who doesn't already know us bothers to introduce themselves. I wonder how long it will take to become connected here.

We're among the first to leave. On our drive home, we discuss the message, which continues during lunch and into the afternoon. At least the sermon sparked conversation, even if we aren't in full agreement.

I also bring up another topic. "When we started, you said excellence in music was important. I think they fall short."

My wife sighs. "I agree." She says nothing more. I think she's willing to overlook this, happy they didn't dodge a social issue.

Two weeks later we return. Yesterday was the Fourth of July. A holiday weekend is never an ideal time to visit a church, especially in the summer. Attendance is usually sparse, and the service is often atypical. Many churches don't even bother to bring their A game, giving their regular leaders the day off and using other people to lead worship and give the message. The result often disappoints. That's what I expect today.

I'm still contemplating the minister's last message we heard. As I review his words, I'm less inclined to agree that he found the midpoint he claimed on this polarizing issue. Though close, he still landed right of center, drawing a line that errs on the side of judgment over love. I opt for love over judgment.

Yet another phrase he said also gives me pause. He called himself a "recovering Baptist." People laughed, and I did too. Though I can claim the same label, my issues run deeper. True, I met my bride at a Baptist church. That was the good part. I only spent five years there, but it was several years too many. I might call myself a "penitent Baptist."

I wonder how much of this man's past has stayed with him. How many other like-minded thinkers have congregated here with him?

With a 10:30 starting time, I have too much time before church, accomplishing all I want to and wondering how to fill the remaining time. For her part, my wife sleeps in and must hurry to get around. By the time we leave, a conflict arises. Though the issue is trivial and soon forgotten, our clash causes a disconnect between us and going to church. As I drive, we both want the other to pray for our experience there. Eventually Candy does. It is a good prayer, and by the time she utters the "amen," my soul is centered and my outlook, right.

Once again, we use the GPS to guide our path. It's a good thing, for without it, I would have missed a critical turn. We pull into the lot five minutes early and are the eighth car. Attendance will be light this holiday weekend.

Practice is still in progress when we arrive. There's a different worship leader than last time and about half the team has changed too. Their sound is rough, bordering on raw. Candy blames the dissonance on poor mixing at the soundboard. I think she's generous in her assessment. The service begins shortly after they finish their run-through of the final song.

Like last time, we sing for twenty-five minutes, with the offering song tucked in the middle. This week, however, they have us break into groups of about six or so to pray about their budgeting process. A key issue is their desire to add an outreach element to their financial plan. I applaud this, at the same time wondering why they need to add it. Their expenses are low, so investing in outreach should have been part of their process for several years.

Though I like to pray, I'm uncomfortable being part of it today. I'm a visitor. I don't know these folks. My preference is to observe, but that's not an option. Soon a group forms around us. A couple Candy knows come to where we sit. They don't ask if we want to pray or if they can join us, they assume it's okay. And it should be. This will stretch me, but I know it will be good for me. Their three granddaughters join us. The wife opens. After some silence, I go next, and then Candy. Perhaps uncomfortable praying in front of two strangers, the girls decline. The husband wraps up.

Some groups are finished praying but not all. We talk for a few minutes as we wait. Once everyone finishes, we sing some more. The teaching elder comes up and the worship leader prays for him. Today, he resumes their series on Philippians, chapter 2, verses 1 through 4.

The theme is unity, a team spirit, "esprit de corps." I jot notes but log nothing new. I end up with three points, complete with alliterated labels, and several bulleted subpoints. Because of our time spent praying and the extra singing, the message is shorter than last time. And the pastor cuts out a video he intended to show. When he finishes, another elder gives the benediction, just like last time.

Today, since it's the first Sunday of the month, they're having their regular monthly potluck. They invite us to stay. We, of course, aren't prepared and have nothing to share.

Part of me wants to leave, but I'm also hungry—both for food and for connection.

I realize great community often occurs around a shared meal. We decide to stay. I stow our Bibles and notebooks in the car while Candy uses the restroom. I finish before she does, standing alone in pathetic solitude. Everyone else is talking. I am not.

Eventually someone takes pity on me and introduces himself. Aside from Candy's friends, he's the first new person I've met. We struggle in conversation, but we both strive to make it work. Eventually Candy joins us, and I introduce her to him. She carries the conversation.

I notice people in the next room, standing in a circle and holding hands. Before we can join them, the prayer for the meal is over. We're among the last to get in line for our food. But there's plenty. The couple we prayed with invite us to sit with them. We talk and eat, sharing life with one another. The wife mentions an email list for communication. She asks tentatively if we'd like to be added. Candy jots our email addresses on a piece of paper for her.

Having implied an interest in becoming more involved with their church, they share details. First, there's no membership. If we want to be regularly involved, we simply tell them, and they add our names to their roster. They offer us a copy, and I'm eager to have one. It will help me learn names. There are eighteen family units listed. And I guess some people who attend aren't included for whatever reason.

Next month is church camp. It's a weeklong event of family camping. "Do you like to camp?"

"I'm not a camper," says Candy, "I'm a 'hotel-er,' but Peter might be interested."

My camping days are over. I prefer to stay home, in my house.

"Most of us aren't campers either," the wife replies with a smile, "but we do like to spend time together. It's so worth it."

"Can we come up for the day or an evening?" Candy asks.

"Sure, that would be fine," the wife confirms as her husband nods. "There will be no community luncheon next month; we'll all be at camp. There will be no church here, either."

The four of us talk some more. Candy and I feel embraced and included. We have made tentative steps to become part of their community, yet we haven't yet talked about it ourselves. *Is The Church That Meets in a School still under consideration? Does Candy want us to go back there? I hope not.*

We help pick up the chairs and tables. When we've done our part, we head out.

After her Sunday afternoon nap, Candy asks me what I think about the church. We discuss their music and the message. We talk about the people and how she knows several, but I know only one. I'm hesitant. "What if there's a church I like better?"

"It doesn't matter," she retorts. "I get to pick, remember? You promised!"

I clarify. "What if there's a church *we* like better?"

"Then we'll deal with it if that time comes."

"So, this is what you want?"

She nods.

"Okay," I say. This isn't quite what I wanted, but it offers many things I like. It isn't like today's typical church, perhaps deviating from it as much as is possible for this generation. They might be as close to the early church as I'll ever get. "But let's ease into it."

Candy nods.

Our search is over. I think.

Takeaway: Sharing a meal is an ideal way to connect with others and form community.

PLUGGING IN

CONNECTING AT THE NONCONVENTIONAL CHURCH

We're back the next Sunday. This is our new church home. With a smaller attendance, it takes little time for us to learn people's names and even less to recognize faces.

As I mentioned, the church is about thirty years old with many three-generation families attending. Most attendees have been part of this church for at least twenty years. They have a deep history together. I wonder how long it'll take for us to fit in that well. But I fear we never will and worry we'll always be on the periphery looking in.

Yet that's not an excuse to not try. I'll give it my best.

When church is over each week, no one leaves—unless they have a time-critical commitment they need to run off to. Most linger in community. I like that. We linger with them. Most weeks we're among the last to leave.

One week the teaching elder shares an insight that resonates with me. He says that some people go to church to worship God and put up with a sermon. Whereas others go for the message and put up with the music.

At various times in my life, I've been both these people. But now I'm neither. I don't go to church for the music or the message, but for a chance to experience meaningful spiritual community when the service ends.

Many years ago, I told our minister that what happened *after* the service was the most significant part to me. Though the church provided uplifting music and inspiring messages, both paled compared to connecting with others in Jesus's name before and after the service.

He shrugged and simply said, "Then just show up when the service is over." Though I never did, the idea intrigued me. It still does.

Ironically, as an introvert, I struggle to interact with others. Staying after church to talk with people and experience spiritual community is difficult for me, despite being intentional about it. Often, I squirm in discomfort and experience too many embarrassing moments.

Yet I persist. Forming a spiritual community and making meaningful connections is worth a bit of personal discomfort.

To connect with this church and its people, I need to stretch myself. This is how I'll experience spiritual community. Eventually I'll become one of them, I just don't know how long it will take.

Candy soon sings backup vocals with their worship team on some Sundays. She's done this before at other churches and relishes the opportunity to do it again.

As for me, I don't see a place to plug in. But when they

decide to offer a prayer team to pray for others after the service, I jump at the chance. Yet we have no takers, and after a few weeks they abandon it as a failed experiment.

Even so, my post-church interactions sometimes give me a chance to pray for people, and I gladly do.

Takeaway: Seek ways to help new people plug in to your church and become accepted by everyone else.

THE POSTCARD CHURCH
THE ALLURE OF SOMETHING FRESH

After a year or so of attending *The Nonconventional Church*, we receive a series of captivating postcards about a new church that will soon launch in our community. I'm intrigued and want to learn more. My wife doesn't. Though they're part of a denomination, I'm willing to overlook that fact if they deliver what they promise. But their denominational affiliation is a sticking point for Candy. I get that.

So, we continue to attend *The Nonconventional Church*. I like everything about it and what they do—except for their music and their message. Neither draws me. Yet the allure of post-service community calls me.

I especially like the monthly potluck. I most anticipate sharing a meal with other believers and sharing life with them around the table. It's the highlight of my month. Seriously.

Yet the food prep falls to my bride, and she wearies of it,

which I comprehend. When she complains, I offer to handle it, but we both know that's a bad idea. It's her kitchen, and I need to stay out of it when she's around.

Though I ably make meals when she isn't present, the outcome is never good if she's there to watch what I do. And the only time I could prepare for our Sunday potluck is when she's home. So, she continues to handle it, but it becomes a growing point of contention.

The part I like best about our church is the part she likes the least.

A few years later, our daughter-in-law surprises us by saying she wants to visit *The Postcard Church*. She invites us to go with them. I know how hard it is to visit a new church, and I sense she's looking for some support on their first visit.

With the pressures of work, life, and a growing family, their church attendance has become sporadic. Though they call *The Rural Church* their church home, they seldom go anymore. I think it's been months.

The Postcard Church is in our community, meeting in the local middle school. Based entirely on their marketing materials, I'm excited to see what we'll encounter. Our daughter-in-law's invitation is an excuse to visit this church and an opportunity for us to encourage our kids to plug back into a faith community. We gladly take a one-week break from our church to help our kids find a spiritual place where they can belong.

Interestingly, *The Postcard Church* is a site plant of the

parent church behind *The Multisite Church*. This is another location. This is also the church that approached *The Traditional Denominational Church* seeking to work with them to expand their outreach to the community. In the end, that church turned them down, opting to continue pursuing their own path.

The Postcard Church is three-quarters of a mile from our home. Though we could walk, we opt to drive. We'll meet our children and grandchildren there.

The church is a satellite location of an established church in the area. Unlike most satellite churches, they offer the music and message live. Their parent church provides centralized governance and financial oversight.

They meet at the local middle school, an arrangement I applaud. Instead of investing money in a building that's only fully used a few hours each week and only fractionally used during business hours, they free up money to invest in outreach and ministry.

Though they pay a rental fee, that's much less than the cost to own and maintain a building. Besides the cost element, this arrangement provides flexibility if they outgrow the space.

As we drive up, the church's trailer sits alongside the driveway, smartly doubling as a sign for the church and signaling the proper entrance. Renting space from a school means they need to set up and tear down each Sunday. The large trailer doubles as a transportation unit on Sunday and storage space throughout the week for their equipment and supplies.

We drive past the trailer. A large vertical welcome banner shows us where to park and which entrance to use, staffed with two smiling greeters.

We talk a bit. Once inside there's no question about where to go. A portable sign tells us to turn right for the service, though the nursery and some children's programs are to the left. We veer right and find ourselves in a large open space, with people mingling about.

As we move forward, two men interrupt their conversation to talk to us, something I seldom witness at the churches we visit. They share their names, and we give ours, connecting with them as we do. After a while we thank them for their time and move into the worship space, a typical middle school gym.

In the middle are folding chairs set in three sections, with one hundred chairs per section. We sit as we wait for the rest of our family to arrive, which they soon do. With the overhead lights off, we rely on indirect lighting. The subdued ambiance pleases but makes it hard to read the literature they gave us.

People and excitement fill the space. All age groups show up, but most are younger than us. It's likely many of the tweens and younger teenagers also attend this school during the week, while their younger siblings will in a few years.

As we wait, soft music plays in the background. People talk with friends. The atmosphere strikes a pleasing balance between churches whose members sit in stoic silence waiting for the service to start and those where frenzied activity overwhelms.

A worship team of five gathers in front. There is a drummer, two on guitars, one on keys, and one backup vocalist. They have no one for bass. The keyboardist doubles as the worship leader. Four-fifths of their ensemble fit within the millennial generation, with a lone baby boomer.

After the first song, the teaching pastor welcomes us and gives announcements. One is a chance to get to know others in the church. The idea is simple: three individuals or families get together three times over three months around a shared meal, dessert, or coffee. This helps people get to know others and form connections. It's a short-term commitment with a long-term benefit.

The pastor moves us into the greeting time. I interact with four people, but no one else makes any effort. I fidget, longing for this time to end. As church greetings go, this one is neither memorable nor haunting.

Our space is now over half full, which is good for a holiday weekend. We sing some more. I don't know any of the songs, but I pick up the chorus on most and the verses on a few.

Next is the offering. There's an information card to fill out and drop in the offering basket, but Candy's still working on it when the offering gets to us. We'll turn it in later. After the collection they slide smoothly into a final song before the sermon.

Despite some empty spaces in the front, they've stealthily added more chairs in the back, which are now mostly full. I suspect the attendance pushes three hundred, with a hundred or more kids and their leaders elsewhere in the facility.

It's week three of a three-part series: "Belong, Believe, Become." Today is about *becoming.* As I contemplate his teaching, I jot down a profound phrase: "Know your community." This makes sense. If we're going to reach our neighbors, we need to better understand them.

He gives us a simple three-point process to engage people: Step one is to talk to them. Step two is to ask them a question. Step three is to invite them for a meal, an outing, or a service opportunity. Most people are open to an invitation to do something.

He concludes with an encouragement to build church where we are.

The service ends. Many people pick up their chair, collapse it, and stow it on a nearby rack. Others come up to us to talk. We enjoy these conversations, which are friendly and engaging.

After doing my part to pick up our family's chairs, we move back into the lobby. There we turn in our information cards to the visitor center and enjoy an extended time of conversation with a most engaging woman.

She tells us about the church. I ask how next Sunday's service will compare to this holiday weekend experience. The woman says the service will be the same format, but there will be many more people. I wonder how many more.

We could return next week to find out. In two weeks, they'll have an after-church event for people who want to learn more about their gathering. This church has much to offer, but we'll miss it since we'll be back at *The Nonconventional Church*.

I long to go to church in my community and attend with my neighbors. This church meets the first criteria, but I don't spot any neighbors.

The four of us debrief at lunch. We all had a positive experience. Our grandson, however, struggled in nursery, with the director of children's programming holding him the entire time. The two of them bonded, which so touched his mother's heart.

"We're coming back next week," she announces. "Do you want to come with us?"

We agree.

Takeaway: Giving first-time visitors a positive experience is key to having them come back.

SETTLING IN
EMBRACING THE POSTCARD CHURCH

W hat started as a one-time visit to *The Postcard Church* turned into a second trip, which became our new normal. It was shockingly easy, and with little discussion, to switch churches. I explained what happened—the best I could—to friends at *The Nonconventional Church*. I'm not sure if they understood or just accepted what I said.

It turns out to be a wise move to make this change so we can attend church with our children and their children. Our daughter-in-law shares that there are some Sundays when they want to stay home, but since they know we're waiting for them at church, they come. It isn't long before the habit of going to church reemerges in their lives.

This is a solemn reminder that just as we can form the habit of going to church, we can also form the habit of not going. Though church attendance isn't the goal, being in intentional spiritual community is. If this happens at church on Sunday mornings, great. If not, seek it elsewhere.

The church offers many community events to let us connect with and reach out to our neighbors. Candy and I take part every chance we get. They offer these merely to serve and to meet, without expectation. I've never been part of a church that was so intentional about reaching out into their community. Their focus feels so right.

I also volunteer to serve as a greeter. My goal is to make eye contact, smile, and give a quick welcome as each person passes by. Though I often struggle with longer conversations, serving as a greeter is an ideal fit for my personality. Candy, who enjoys talking with others, is a perfect fit for the visitor center. This is where she shines. She also sometimes helps prepare the weekly bank deposit after the offering.

Our kids volunteer as greeters, as well as serving in the children's ministry. Our grandchildren at times help their parents or grandfather greet people as they arrive at church. It's a family effort.

It's not long before the church switches from one Sunday service to two.

We also discover some of our neighbors go to the church with us. I look for them each Sunday and try to connect every chance I get.

I develop a practice of walking to church. Praying as I go, the fifteen-minute stroll prepares me for my morning experience. I do this unless it's raining or the path is icy. Candy drives. This means we have transportation for post-church activity with family, which usually involves going out for lunch.

Takeaway: Make it easy for people to find the right place to serve in your church. It should focus on their strengths and interests, not on your needs or open positions. Cajoling them to serve out of a sense of duty or guilt benefits no one.

THINGS CHANGE
A WRINKLE AT THE POSTCARD CHURCH

We all enjoy attending *The Postcard Church*: Candy and I, our son and daughter-in-law, and our grandkids. Each of us likes it and looks forward to it every week. Connections turn into relationships. We worship God and serve him in our community with our neighbors. I dismiss the fact that they are part of a denomination as a nonissue that doesn't affect me—or does it?

The denomination leadership starts making politically correct pronouncements at the expense of core perspectives they once valued—or at least what I thought they once valued. It grates on me. Yet I don't see it reflected in our Sunday morning experiences, so I overlook it.

Though my wife ignores it, too, our daughter-in-law asks how I can go to a church I don't agree with. Though she knows my heart, she wonders if my presence silently endorses the denomination's position. It's a good question, one which I can't resolve. So, we continue to attend each week, even as we see these areas of disconnect occasionally slip into their messaging.

Our son, however, carries more concern. After prayerful deliberation, he and his wife decide they can't continue attending *The Postcard Church*. When they tell their kids they'll start going to a different one, the first, and only, question out of the little ones' mouths is, "Will Grandpa and Grandma go with us to the new church?"

The right answer, the only answer, is "Yes!"

The Church with Much to Offer—which we visited early on in our search and offered many intriguing opportunities—recently announced they'd bought a building in our community and would remodel it to accommodate hundreds of people for multiple services each Sunday.

This local presence appeals to us, and we decide to attend *The Church with Much to Offer* at their main location until they open this secondary one. We'll need only wait a few months.

Expecting this change, our son and daughter-in-law had completed their service commitments at *The Postcard Church*. This frees them to make an immediate switch. Candy and I, however, still have some assignments to complete. It will be several weeks before we can join our family at *The Church with Much to Offer*.

We share this decision with a few people at *The Postcard Church* but not many. Our plan is to slide away quietly without raising concerns or creating problems.

I've too often seen disgruntled parishioners light a fuse on some contentious issue and then leave in a huff, letting others deal with the fallout they created. I've seen this destroy churches.

Takeaway: If you must separate from your church, consider the best way to do so. Leave on as good of terms as possible, and don't cause problems. They are part of Jesus's church, so do nothing to harm them.

A CHANGE IN PLANS

RETURNING TO THE CHURCH WITH MUCH TO OFFER

Though we allow enough time to drive to church, we don't factor in extra time. The facility isn't at all what I remember. We turn in the first drive but all the spaces in that lot are full. We follow a road around the back of the building and discover a much larger lot on the other side. It's full, too, with many cars parked in the grass. Eventually we find a space, but it's far from the entrance.

By the time we hike to the main doors, we're late. Greeters enthusiastically welcome us with broad smiles and infectious hospitality. Their cheerful demeanor helps me shake off my dismay over being late.

Once inside, however, we need to navigate our way to the sanctuary.

Though an open space, with much room, it's quite congested. Some people are still leaving from the second service, while others—like us—are late for the third. Signs point us in the right direction, and we join the crowd headed toward the sanctuary. I spot doors to the balcony and figure it's our best option. At the same time, Candy follows the arrow pointing down a staircase to reach the main part of the sanctuary. I follow.

The place is mostly full, but we find space for two. They're still going through the welcome and opening announcements. The first thing I hear is that they'll offer six Christmas Eve services. This boggles my mind. I've never heard of the need for that many services.

I estimate the sanctuary and balcony might seat between 1,000 and 1,200 people. This is far different from my recollection of several hundred on our last visit. I grapple with the disconnect between my memory and this experience, but I shove it aside.

A worship team of twelve leads us in three songs. Though unfamiliar to me, their energetic playing leads us into worship. Thankfully, God's answer to our pre-church prayer allows me to fully engage in what's happening now, with no self-reproach for arriving late.

The minister opens his message with the thought-provoking question, "What are you clinging to?" I contemplate the question for too long and miss what comes next, unable to connect it with the main part of the sermon.

He pulls me back in when he says, "The point of the Bible is to point us to Jesus." I heartily agree.

The minister's text, from Hebrews 7:1–19, talks about Melchizedek. We first encounter him in the Old Testament, Genesis 14:17–24. He foreshadows Jesus and his work. Though Jesus isn't from the priestly line of Aaron, he serves as a new kind of priest and will be a priest forever. This is who we'll celebrate during this Advent season: Jesus coming to earth to be our priest and to save us.

After the service, Candy and I head to the visitor center, while our kids go to retrieve their children from their respective places. After we give them our contact information and receive their literature, we find the rest of our family.

We leave to eat lunch together and discuss our new church home.

Takeaway: What people experience making their way into the church sanctuary influences what they'll experience during the service. Don't focus so much on the service that you lose sight of what happens before.

MOVING FORWARD

EMBRACING THE CHURCH WITH MUCH TO OFFER

The reason our return to *The Church with Much to Offer* so confused me is that they added to their facility since our first visit a few years ago. Their original space, a nicely finished gymnasium, does indeed accommodate hundreds, while their new sanctuary, with balcony, seats many more. The gymnasium serves as overflow space for the services.

The plan for a second location near where we live falls through. They make a couple more false starts in our community and seem to be on indefinite hold. But I'm ready to help when the time comes . . . if the time comes.

Mindful of my pledge to not overcommit, I'm looking for one place to serve at church where I can help others. Though I have experience in many areas, I don't feel God's call to repeat them. Instead, I feel a pull to simplicity where I can connect with others. I'm open to serve as a greeter or be on their prayer team. I've done both in the past and want to do so again.

But being a greeter or serving on the prayer team would both happen as part of the Sunday service. That means being open to serve in one other area. So far, I don't know what that is.

I place that decision on hold, waiting for them to launch a site near where we live.

However, I don't know when or if it will happen. But I know they need to do something—either here or someplace else.

As we await their move into our community, we continue to attend the main location with our son and his family. On Sundays when our son's family is out of town, we go to church with our daughter and her family. And on those rare occasions when neither are available, we go to *The Mega Church*, but that's only happened twice. So, we focus on *The Church with Much to Offer.*

They move to four services to accommodate all the people who want to attend. For the middle two services we can gather in the main sanctuary or the gymnasium, which has its own worship team and provides the sermon via video feed. I prefer the open and much-less-congested gym, but I'm the only one in my family who does. We do, however, attend in the gym, with several hundred others. This frees up space in the main sanctuary for visitors.

They're planning another addition, too, but it's not expanding the sanctuary, so I'm not sure how it will address Sunday mornings with a collective attendance of several thousand.

Overall, it's an exciting church to attend, and there's much spiritual vitality—the best I've experienced at any church in the area. Yet we haven't made many meaningful connections. I've been holding off, waiting for what they hope to do in our community. But I need to move forward the best I can with the options before me now.

I steadfastly hope to go to church in our community, worshiping and serving with our neighbors. My prayer is for that to occur and that *The Church with Much to Offer* will provide it.

I don't know what will happen, but God does. And that's good enough for me.

Takeaway: We must do all we can so that our church best serves God and advances his kingdom, while at the same time trusting him with the outcome.

If you liked *Shopping for Church,* please leave a review online. Your review will help others discover this book and encourage them to read it too. Thank you.

BOOKS IN THE VISITING CHURCHES SERIES

Other books in the Visiting Churches Series:

- 52 Churches
- More Than 52 Churches
- Visiting Online Church
- The 52 Churches Workbook
- The More Than 52 Churches Workbook

For a list of all Peter's books, go to
PeterDeHaan.com/books.

FOR SMALL GROUPS, SUNDAY SCHOOL, AND CLASSES

Shopping for Church makes an ideal discussion guide for small groups, Sunday School, and classes. In preparation for the conversation, read one chapter of this book before you meet.

When you get together, pray and ask for Holy Spirit insight.

Discuss the key points of the chapter and explore the takeaway item.

- Celebrate areas your church does well.
- Consider a weakness that needs improvement.
- Determine what you can do to bring about positive change.

End by asking God to help you apply what you've learned.

May God bless you as you discuss this book and explore how to apply it to your practices.

ABOUT PETER DEHAAN

Peter DeHaan, PhD, wants to change the world one word at a time. His books and blog posts discuss God, the Bible, and church, geared toward spiritual seekers and church dropouts. Many people feel church has let them down, and Peter seeks to encourage them as they search for a place to belong.

But he's not afraid to ask tough questions or make religious people squirm. He's not trying to be provocative. Instead, he seeks truth, even if it makes people uncomfortable. Peter urges Christians to push past the status quo and reexamine how they practice their faith in every part of their lives.

Peter earned his doctorate, awarded with high distinction, from Trinity College of the Bible and Theological Seminary. He lives with his wife in beautiful Southwest Michigan and wrangles crossword puzzles in his spare time.

A lifelong student of Scripture, Peter wrote the 1,000-page website ABibleADay.com to encourage people to explore the Bible, the greatest book ever written. His popular blog, at PeterDeHaan.com, addresses biblical Christianity to build a faith that matters.

Read his blog, receive his newsletter, and learn more at PeterDeHaan.com.

BOOKS BY PETER DEHAAN

Visiting Churches Series

52 Churches

The 52 Churches Workbook

More Than 52 Churches

The More Than 52 Churches Workbook

Visiting Online Church

Shopping for Church

40-Day Bible Study Series

Dear Theophilus (the Gospel of Luke)

Acts Bible Study

Isaiah Bible Study

Minor Prophets Bible Study

Job Bible Study

Living Water (John)

Love Is Patient (1 and 2 Corinthians)

Revelation Bible Study

1, 2, & 3 John Bible Study

Hebrews Bible Study

James and Jude Bible Study

Matthew Bible Study

1 & 2 Peter Bible Study

Mark Bible Study

Holiday Celebration Devotionals

The Advent of Jesus

The Passion of Jesus (Lent)

The Victory of Jesus (Easter)

The Ministry of Jesus

Thanksgiving with Jesus

New Year with Jesus

Bible Character Sketches Series

Women of the Bible

The Friends and Foes of Jesus

Old Testament Sinners and Saints

More Old Testament Sinners and Saints

Heroes and Heavies of the Apocrypha

200 Old Testament Sinners and Saints

Other Books

Elephant God

Jesus's Broken Church

Martin Luther's 95 Theses (formerly *95 Tweets*)

The Christian Church's LGBTQ Failure

Bridging the Sacred-Secular Divide (formerly *Woodpecker Wars*)

Beyond Psalm 150

How Big Is Your Tent?

For the latest list of all Peter's books, go to
PeterDeHaan.com/books.

www.ingramcontent.com/pod-product-compliance
Lightning Source LLC
Chambersburg PA
CBHW060505130626
46553CB00002B/414